Born To Lose
Bound To Win

*The Amazing Journey
of Mother Eliza George*

Lorry Lutz

Harvest House Publishers
Irvine, California 92714

> Dedicated to Allen Finley
> President of Christian Nationals
> who never doubted that
> this story must be told
> and
> my beloved husband, Allen,
> who had faith to believe I could tell it.

Acknowledgements

My deepest gratitude is expressed to Cecelia Davis, Mother's adopted daughter, for helping so graciously in the initial research; to Gus and Otheliah Marwieh, Mother's spiritual children, for countless hours of interviews and helpful corrections; to the many friends in Liberia who made Mother's life come alive for me; to Elle Mae Rundle and others of the "Eliza Davis-George Clubs" who shared her story; to my secretaries, Carolyn Garner and Marilyn Mote for their faithful help; to Ruth Finley who so cheerfully traveled with me to Liberia to help unearth the story. And for the many others whom I cannot name who helped me piece together the amazing life of Mother Eliza Davis George.

BORN TO LOSE, BOUND TO WIN

Copyright © 1980 by Christian Nationals Evangelism Commission, Inc.

Published by Harvest House Publishers
Irvine, California 92714

Library of Congress Catalog Card Number 80-83877
ISBN 0-89081-274-8

All rights reserved. No portion of this book may be reproduced in any form without the written permission of the Publisher.

Printed in the United States of America.

Contents

Foreword..................................6
1. The Surging Surf 7
2. Life in Liberia 15
3. The Endless Walk 19
4. After Slavery 23
5. The Year 1900 31
6. The Love of Liberty 39
7. One Breath from Death 51
8. Mr. and Mrs. 67
9. Why Did You Wait So Long? 73
10. Coming Home 79
11. Cerella............................85
12. Strength and Sorrow 91
13. Born in a Cassava Patch 97
14. The Dream 101
15. Mother on the Rock 107
16. Go and Sin No More 113
17. The Living Newspaper 119
18. Who Will Tell Me of God? 127
19. Retired from Duty? 133
20. Big Plans 143
21. The "Cursed" Place 147
22. Son, Let's Pray 151
23. The Jeep and the Journey 157
24. Romance in San Francisco 161
25. Mother Picks a Wife 165
26. Son, Take It 169
27. The Tribal Reunion 173
28. Back to the Jungle 181
29. Lights to Share 187
30. Year 100 193

Foreword
by Sherwood Eliot Wirt

Mother Eliza Davis-George. What a beautiful person! To know her was to sense all over again the infinite capacities of the human spirit when touched by the Spirit of God.

A poor little "colored" girl growing up in segregated Texas, she made the "mistake" of taking seriously the stories she learned in Sunday School. She literally wanted the world to know about Jesus, and sought to be used of God to that end. When the religious establishment set out to correct her visionary ideas, she found that she had to choose between the "important" people and Jesus. She chose Jesus, went to Africa on a shoestring, and without any portfolio, any support agency beyond a few friends, any anything, she won her way. One by one the barriers of sex, color, status, funding, toppled before her. One woman with God proved more than either American or Africa could handle.

She went to the heads of government and wheedled gifts of land out of them without a single influential person representing or sponsoring her.

She pulled a naked little boy out of the bush, put pants on him and enrolled him in her school. Today he holds a graduate degree from the Golden Gate Seminary in California and is one of Liberia's notable Christian educators and statesmen.

She came back to Texas and raised money where there was no money to raise. She sent every penny of it to Africa and followed it to see that it was properly spent.

She lived to be a hundred, and when she died full of years, her faith in Jesus was as strong as ever.

Eliza Davis-George. You will love her story as Lorry tells it so effectively in these pages. Eliza belongs with the heroes of the faith, one of God's quiet people who left the human race better than she found it. God rest her soul.

chapter one

The Surging Surf

The surging surf tossed the rowboat as though it were a piece of cork. The sea was treacherous along this part of the Liberian coast, but for centuries Kru tribesmen had faced the sea's furies in these time-proven vessels.

Hauling out the day's catch in their hand-sewn nets, two Krus fishermen were preparing to pull the boat up on the beach for the night. Their village was hidden in the jungle, which hugged the shore as closely as the ocean would permit—the surging tide and the relentless jungle meeting at an impasse. Darkness fell suddenly here on the equator, and they were eager to get home before the trail was engulfed in night.

The Krus were chatting amiably over their catch when they spotted three figures moving along the shore—a rare sight along this desolate coast. As the three drew closer the men were startled to see a "civilized" woman and two young boys plodding in the sand. She was not a tribal woman, for she wore a Western dress of dark print, heavy boots, and a safari helmet. She carried a long stick in her right hand, which she used to pull herself forward. The barefoot boys, dressed only in a pair of tattered shorts, walked behind her, where the receding tide washed over their feet to cool them from the sun-baked sand.

The men stopped their work to watch the unlikely trio approaching them, wondering what they were doing so many miles from the nearest settlement of Americo-Liberians—so named after the freed American slaves who had colonized this land more than a hundred years earlier.

The woman was taller than the Krus were, and carried herself erect even in the soft surf and shifting sand. She wiped the perspiration from her face and neck, and in spite of her obvious fatigue gave them a cheerful smile which lit up her warm brown face. Now that she was within speaking distance, they could see that she was no longer young, but since the fishermen didn't know how old they themselves were, they did not think of her in terms of age.

The two boys trailing her looked as though they would soon enter manhood, though they were both a good head shorter than the woman. One of the boys carried a canvas bag over his arm.

Calling out in English, which the Krus understood because of their contacts with "civilized" towns along the coast, the woman greeted them.

"Where you come from, Mama?" one of the fishermen asked. "You far from home out here."

"Son, we've been walking all day. We left Greenville before daybreak this morning. I'm Mother Eliza Davis George, and these are two of my boys, Robert and Tussnah. We are on our way to Monrovia."

"Monrovia! You going to walk there?" the astonished fishermen asked. "Why, it takes more than three days by rowboat. How you gonna walk that far?"

Mother Eliza* stood resting her weight on her walking stick and wiped her perspiring face and neck once again. "The Lord will help us, son. But tell me, how far is it to the next village? I think Robert and Tussnah are getting too tired to walk much farther tonight."

"The next civilized settlement is across the Sehnkwehn River," one of the men answered, "but you can't cross tonight. It's high tide. We could take you over tomorrow if you would like to stay in our village tonight."

At the offer of traditional tribal hospitality, the boys' faces broke into a grin, for they knew this meant a good meal of rice and fish cooked in palm butter, and a mat on the floor of one of the huts in the village. They had grown up in just such a village before they came to Mother's mission school, and they

---

*Mother Eliza Davis George's close friends often called her "Mother George." However, in this book she will usually be designated as "Mother Eliza."

remembered how often their own mothers had cooked for strangers walking through the jungle from another town.

Without a moment's hesitation Mother Eliza accepted the offer; she had spent many a night in an African hut, sharing the simple fare with these hospitable tribal people since she had come to Africa from Texas 26 years earlier. A grass mat on a dirt floor would be luxury compared to the unprotected beach with its stinging sand!

For a moment she almost forgot the pressure urging her forward on her 200-mile walk to Monrovia. It would take at least five more days like this one—days of 100-degree temperature under a relentless sun, days of burning feet and parched throat, days of pushing her 51-year-old body to the very limit of endurance. From other trips by dugout canoe along this same shore she knew there were dozens of rivers and streams rushing into the ocean between here and Monrovia, and each one would take courage and ingenuity to cross.

But for tonight God had provided a friendly village, a meal, and a sheltered place to sleep. And before the startled Krus had a chance to lead the way to the village, she dropped on her knees, saying, "Children, let's pray and thank God for bringing us this far."

The next morning dawned bright, clear, and hot. But Eliza and the boys had slept a dreamless sleep on the floor of the chief's hut, untroubled by the scampering rats or voracious mosquitoes. They felt rested and ready for the day ahead. One of the chief's wives gave Eliza some cold cassava and rice to take along on the journey to add to the meager store she had brought in her canvas bag. She filled her jug from the drum of water which her daughters had hauled from the river the night before.

The fishermen led them back to the shore and ferried them along the coast and across the wide Sehnkwehn River, dropping them on the eastern shore. Mother Eliza thanked them profusely, reminding them once more of the Scripture she had taught them the night before as they sat around the fire in the village. "God bless you, my sons, for your kindness to Mother," she called as they pulled away from the shore.

The early hours of the morning were easier to bear, for even though the air was already hot and sultry, there was still an occasional whisper of a breeze off the ocean, and the sands had cooled off during the night. Robert and Tussnah scampered ahead, pushing each other into the surf, as boys will, and picking up unusual shells to bring back for Mother to see.

Riding in the canoe this morning had brought back memories of that voyage from Monrovia to Greenville in 1928, just two years earlier. By steamer it took just a day-and-a-half to make the 200-mile journey, but she recalled how she had begrudged every minute of it. She had been away from her beloved Africa for eight long years, for one obstacle after another had dragged out an interminable furlough. But with what anticipation she had returned! She had urged the ship forward with her very will, so eager was she to get back to Kelton mission, to be with her "children" once again, to visit the villagers and tell them of Christ!

She remembered that everything had gone according to plan; the voyage was uneventful, the seas calm; their crates and boxes had been unloaded quickly in Greenville, and willing porters were recruited for the early-morning trek back to the mission the next day. Mother and her adopted daughter, Maude, walked the four miles to the village of Lexington, where they were royally welcomed by their old friends, the Witherspoons, in whose home they stayed the night. Her husband, C. Thompson George, had disappeared into town for several hours, but had returned by nightfall with a trail of small boys carrying loads on their heads.

But now Mother Eliza was more suitably dressed than the first time she had arrived in Liberia, in 1914. Her dress had short sleeves and an open neck, but her skirts were still long and full, and her rubber boots reached halfway up her calves. She would need them for this day's walk! The pith helmet that was her trademark up and down the jungle trails was the same one she had worn when she left Africa eight years earlier.

A vast swamp blocked their way to the mission, and to go around it would have added at least another day's walk. So Mother led the way, checking each step with her long staff, and looking for all the world like Mrs. Moses leading her people to the promised land.

The journey was difficult. Mosquitoes and tsetse flies buzzed around the porters' sweating bodies, becoming more irritating as the heat of the day increased. Instinctively the Krus kept a wary eye for the deadly green mamba snakes, which lived in the lower branches of the trees and could attack with lightning speed when disturbed.

Mother Eliza didn't know what to expect when she arrived at the mission. Though only eight miles inland from Lexington, little news came from the inland area, and her friends in the town knew nothing about the condition of the mission.

Mr. George had been rather vague in describing what he had accomplished on the new house before he had joined her for furlough in the U.S.A. He had told her that he and the boys had sawed and prepared about a thousand planks for building, and that the foundation of heavy "Warner blocks" had been set and the framework put up.

"With the supplies and tools we've brought with us now, it shouldn't take us more than a few weeks to finish the house," he had assured Eliza. "We can stay in the old thatched hut until then, since most of the children haven't come back to school yet."

It was a relief to emerge from the swamp and to set their feet on a solid trail overhung with jungle vines, and heavily shaded by umbrella and cork trees.

Wading across a brackish creek that seeped away into the underbrush, Mother came to a fork in the trail and instinctively turned toward the mission. Suddenly she saw a young African coming toward her. He seemed familiar, and she put her hand up over her eyes to shield them from the blinding sun.

"Why, son, son—can this be little Jimmy? I don't believe it—you've grown so tall." Turning, she called back along the trail, "Mr. George, come here. Look who's come to welcome us." And then in her typical fashion, she put her hand on Jimmy's shoulder and, closing her eyes, with her face turned into the brilliant African sunshine, she prayed:

> Dear Lord, now thank You for bringing us here today. Thank you for keeping Jimmy safe these many long years we've been away. May we praise Your name as we endeavor to serve You among these precious native people who need to know Your love. Amen.

"Son, have you come to take us back to the mission with you?" she asked as Father George caught up with them and joined in the happy reunion.

But Jimmy's face, which had been so radiant with happiness at seeing his beloved "parents," fell with apprehension. In later years he would so aptly describe this scene.

"I dropped my face; I frown plenty cause the mission it broke down," I told Mother Eliza. "The bug-a-bugs they eat everything!"

"What do you mean, Jimmy? What about all the planks we sawed and piled up for the house? Surely you don't mean they've been destroyed," Father George asked sharply.

Now apprehensive, Father George took the lead as the little troupe followed him across the last creek before the mission. A desolate sight met their eyes—the termites had indeed destroyed everything. The thatched hut that had been the Georges' first home had fallen upon itself, with the mat walls folding over, broken, brown, and dead. The sagging thatched roof had lost its leaves to the elements, and what was left was covered with jungle growth.

Peering through the window in the one wall that still partially stood, Mother could see the remains of boxes of books and papers that Father had hastily packed before he left, soaked by rains and eaten by the busy working termites. It seemed impossible to imagine that those tiny ants could do so much damage.

But African termites are relentless in their quest for survival. The queen of this matriarchal society may live for 20 years in her dark, dank prison cell, producing up to 30,000 eggs a day. She is fertilized by one termite king through all those years, who is larger than the millions of blind workers they produce, but appears small beside his colossal mate, who has developed into a five-inch, grublike organism made up of blood and ovaries a thousand times heavier than the workers who feed her.

Wherever that prolific queen was hidden, she and her multitudinous army had done their work well, and every paper, book, piece of furniture, plank, footing, and thatch had succumbed to their tireless mandibles. What they had not completely destroyed, the moisture and mold had!

Father and Mother looked at each other in despair; then Mr. George stalked off to check on the piles of lumber he had left stacked for building, Jimmy trailing behind him. The porters sat on their haunches where they had dropped their burdens, watching to see what this God-woman from across the sea would do.

Maude's chin quivered as she looked forlornly around the place she had known as home; what was Mother going to do now? But Mother reached her arms out for the disappointed young girl: "Come here, Maudie—this isn't the end of the world. God has brought us here to do His work, and He'll help us through this."

Then, dropping to her knees and drawing Maude down beside her, Mother presented her petitions once again to her heavenly Father, confident that He would hear her.

Rising from her knees, and determined not to let the children see her discouragement, she called the porters: "Children, we'll just have to turn around and go back to Lexington today, and tomorrow we'll see about buying more material to build the station. If we hurry, we can get through the swamp before dark."

And with determined steps she led the way back to Lexington.

chapter two

Life In Liberia

While Mr. George supervised the hiring of men and purchasing of materials, Eliza began to gather the children together again. Some had married and would never come back to school, while others had lost interest and were content to stay home in their villages. But surprisingly, some parents were now more willing to allow their children to go to the mission than in earlier years, and before many months had passed she even had several little girls in her care.

As soon as Mr. George had a two-room thatch hut completed, Mother and some of the children moved out to Kelton. Aware of the scarcity of food, Mother was eager to get a mission garden planted, and she put even the youngest girls to work hoeing and weeding. Tools were scarce, but the children remembered that Mother always used a big hoe she had brought from the States, while the girls used "pot hoes" (thick sticks) to make rows for planting rice.

Genevieve Mason, who was only ten years old when she moved out to the mission, remembers Mother climbing on top of the roof to help thatch one of the buildings. "There was nothing Mother wouldn't do on the mission. She made herself a real Liberian. She knew that she wasn't able to get her things from home. God even fixed it so that Mother George could eat anything."

Being "Liberian" was the secret not only of her acceptance by the people but of her very survival. Help from the churches in the United States was rare, and the economic conditions in 1929 were to make matters worse! The Georges hadn't expected to have to replace everything on the station when they returned, and the debts piled up faster than they had anticipated.

With so many children coming to the mission, Father George put up a separate boys' house. Though built of thatch siding and roof, it nevertheless required funds for lumber framing and labor. Father George was often harsh with the children, but without his supervision of the boys, the work could never have been accomplished.

Praying for funds from America was part of the daily routine, and when the mail arrived, there was great expectancy. Though their mission sent funds regularly, Mother Eliza recorded in her autobiography two special gifts which arrived that year.

"A letter was received from Mrs. Morris of Mineral Wells, Texas, enclosing a check for $100, half of which was donated by her. She said that she had heard Maude speak when she was in the United States and was interested in our work."

The second gift, of $80, came from her ever-faithful friend, Pastor Pleasants of St. John's Baptist Church in Houston, Texas. A note informing her that the church had decided to take up an offering for Kelton Mission every Tuesday evening was encouraging.

Still, the pressures mounted because the funds were simply not enough to pay the debts, provide food and other necessities, and continue building for the growing work.

It was obvious that someone would have to go back to the United States once again to share the need in the churches. In their isolation, the Georges were not aware of the devastating effects of the 1929 financial crash around the world. Difficult though it was, they decided that Mr. George would return to the U.S.A. while Mother remained to care for the work at Kelton. Remembering the tremendous loss when the mission was left uninhabited before, and not wanting to send the children away again, they dared not both leave.

Even though Father George had been away for almost a year, he had been able to send very little money, and the situation at Kelton had deteriorated.

The children knew that Mother fasted and prayed for funds to take care of the mission, but she never let on the desperation that was beginning to grip her heart.

She bought supplies on credit from every store in Greenville; shopkeepers trusted her and knew the good work she was doing, but now they would extend no more credit.

And "her cupboards were bare." Her supply of rice was almost gone, and the new crop would not be ready for months. She needed staples—flour, sugar, and salt. Most of the children had only the clothes they wore on their backs; few had blankets for the chilly nights of the rainy season.

Many a night Mother cried out to God in desperation:

> O heavenly Father, Thou hast taught us to pray for our daily bread. Lord, thou dost know that I do not have one penny to buy food and pay the workers here at the mission. Father, send us something to meet our needs as Thou hast promised. Help me to keep trusting Thee so that the children will know Thou art caring for them.

Though she encouraged the children to be thankful for their meager meals, it broke her heart to see their thin arms and legs, and to send them to scratch for tasteless roots to add bulk to their monotonous diet.

It had been months since gifts of any kind had reached the mission; in fact, steamers rarely visited the Sinoe port for any reason. The long tentacles of the Wall Street crash had touched the Liberian shores, and not only the mission but the economy of the whole country was suffering.

In spite of the poverty, Mother was determined that the children would not go naked. Though the younger ones would have been delighted to go without clothing in the tropical heat, she made sure that each one was at least minimally clothed. That meant constant patching and mending, and even cutting down her slips and dresses to make something for them.

But the financial crisis continued—until one morning a ship at long last entered the Sinoe port. When Mother Eliza heard that the steamer had stopped at Greenville, she hastily made arrangements to go to town by "ankle express," as she jokingly called the long walk. She took Robert and Tussnah and several of the other younger children with her to help carry groceries, for she was outwardly confident that there would be gifts for the mission in the mail. The rest of the children were excited to see them go, for mail usually meant extra food and parcels of clothing, and it had been a long time since they had had any of that.

They arrived in Greenville late on that Monday afternoon and went straight to the post office. There were a few letters from her family, which Eliza pocketed to be read at her leisure back at the mission. She was relieved to see a letter from her husband, from whom she had not heard for many months. She opened it eagerly, hoping that he had sent some money for her. Her heart sank—nothing! Glancing through his letter, she learned that he had been very ill and had not been able to hold many meetings. But he hastened to assure her, "I'm fine now and have a busy schedule planned."

Then he added a cheering note, "A gift of several hundred dollars has been sent to you by one of the churches that learned of our need. I hope you have received it."

Eliza glanced frantically through the remaining letters in her hand, but there was nothing from a church or from the mission. There was one last letter from the post office in Monrovia. Tearing it open, she read:

> A postal order for $200 has been received for you. Return this form with your signature within 30 days.

But the letter was dated four weeks earlier!

Eliza stood in a little island of despair as the happy and boisterous crowds of Africans pushed past her. Staring at the stark missive in her hand, she couldn't believe what she read.

"Lord, how could this have happened?" she thought. "Who could have made such a mistake to send the money to Monrovia rather than here?" But when she looked at the children who had pressed around her, she was reminded that her heavenly Father loved them more than she did.

Disregarding the people around her, she gathered her little brood of children closer and tried to explain what had happened. "Children, praise God, the money has come; but it isn't here in Greenville. You know, sometimes when God answers prayer, He expects us to do our part too. He has sent the money to Monrovia, and Mother will just have to find a way to get it from there."

Robert was the first to comprehend what she was saying. "But Mother, the steamship is gone, and there won't be one for months again." And then his lip began to tremble as he realized that, steamship or canoe, what did it matter? There was no money to go by any kind of ship to Monrovia, 200 miles up the coast.

But, drawing on that persistent faith which had brought her to Africa against all odds, a plan was beginning to form in Mother's mind. She had never been one to lose heart easily, and with just a little more effort on her part, the money was within her reach. As she herded the little group down the road, she reassured them, "We'll just go and stay with Rev. Burch here in town tonight, and God will show us what to do."

What God was telling her was plain and simple—the only way to get that money was to go to Monrovia; and since she had no money to hire a boat, she would just have to walk!

chapter three

The Endless Walk

Somehow Eliza had never noticed that the sea was so noisy; while sailing across the ocean to Africa there had just been the steady swish-swish as the ship dipped into the rollers, and the sound of the wind whistling around her on the deck. In the evenings she had stood by the rail, straining her eyes into the darkness as if she could see the distant shore of Africa; and the silver moonlight across the water was a peaceful beckoning road to the fulfillment of her dreams.

But here along the shore the ocean roared without ceasing, beating against her ears as no African drum could, as if to drown out her very thoughts.

She was alone with her thoughts, for Robert and Tussnah did what boys do on beaches—they picked up pebbles and driftwood, marveling over a dead blue bottle washed up on shore, balancing themselves precariously on the huge black rocks which God had sculptured on the beach.

And whenever the heat became unbearable they would throw themselves into the surf, laughing and shouting as the waves tumbled them over and over like playful kittens. Eliza knew there were dangerous undertows along this shore, and she watched anxiously whenever they were in the water, shouting over the roar, "Be careful, children!" knowing they could not hear her.

But sometimes the heat became so unbearable, especially at midday, that even Eliza threw herself into the sea, clothes and all. Then the boys would scamper back and throw themselves in to join her, and for a few minutes they would forget the heat and their blistered feet—and the urgency of their journey.

But most of the time Eliza simply trudged along the shore, placing one foot in front of the other, one step closer to Monrovia, to the post office, to the money order which must be waiting for her there.

She found herself thinking back to the first time she had seen the burning sands of Liberia's coastline—and her undignified arrival on it!

"Come on, Mammy!" She could still hear the almost-naked black boy as he reached his hands up to steady Eliza as she looked down the rope ladder hanging from the Celtic's sides into the rough, hand-hewn canoe below.

The Celtic had arrived at Monrovia the morning of January 20, 1914, and had lain three miles out to sea, rocking in the gentle swells and the feverish sun. Eliza's long-sleeved cotton blouse, with the navy bow-tie tucked under her chin and the heavy worsted skirt, had captured the heat. Her cotton undershirt stuck to her body like her grandmother's mustard plasters. Once the ship had struck anchor, the sea breeze, which had been some source of relief from the heat, stopped.

Monrovia in 1914 was little more than a small town, with four to five thousand people. It had been settled by American slaves who had been freed in the early part of the nineteenth century and had tried to carve out a living in the hostile heat and humidity of Liberia. The twin perils of malaria and dysentery took the lives of over half the settlers in those early years.

The only street in Monrovia was really just a winding path overrun with grass and obstructed by rocky outcroppings. Goats, cattle, and sheep grazed among the houses and outbuildings.

Many of the buildings along the street were half-completed, with their owners' ambitious dreams outstripping reality. Grassy outcroppings along the road served as the community laundry, where washing was spread out today. Most of the buildings, whether occupied or half-finished, had a crumbling, weather-beaten look, for anything made of wood or grass survived only a few seasons, as Eliza would later learn, to her sad experience.

But now, trudging along the beach in 1930, Eliza realized that she had felt at home here these 26 years—even this desolate, forbidding coastline was hers—and the tribal people to whom she had come to bring God's message of love were her brothers and sisters. Once again the overwhelming urgency of her journey to

Monrovia gripped her; but even as a surge of despair overwhelmed her, Eliza's indomitable faith surfaced, and she pleaded, "Heavenly Father, You brought me here to tell these native children about You; You know they are hungry and that we have no money. Help me to reach Monrovia in time."

Tussnah and Robert disappeared over the sandy ridge ahead. Eliza had been falling behind them all afternoon. She had taken off her heavy boots so that she could walk in the cooling water. The salt stung the raw blisters which had popped up into fat bubbles on her heels, then burst like bubblegum and were now open and bleeding. But the coolness of the salty water was preferable to the burning sand, which seared the bottoms of her feet.

Eliza seemed to have lost track of time. "Let's see, this must be Wednesday," she mused to herself, the constant roar of the surf drowning out her words. "No, it's Thursday. We left on Tuesday morning before the sun rose—yes, this is the third day. It's Thursday."

Then, as if to defy the incessant pounding of the sea, which had been her constant companion for almost four days, she began singing a song which she had composed the first day on the beach.

> When your path is dark and your heart shrinks
>   with fear,
> When all seems lost and failure seems
>   near,
> Keep a clear, steady mind—just work, watch,
>   and pray;
> Jesus knows, loves, cares, and will your cause
>   defray.
>
> Just keep on, victory is ahead;
> Look to Jesus, who multitudes fed.
> He's the Son of God, the Living Bread;
> He's the Ruler and the great Head.

A daring wave, getting ahead of the tide, suddenly slapped against Mother, almost causing her to lose her balance. As the undertow pulled the sand out from beneath her feet, she steadied herself and kept right on singing, louder than before.

> Just keep on going on when your spirit's low,
> When you've done your best and success seems
>   slow.

> By faith trust His word, keep His righteous
>   command;
> Fill your heart with song, whether on sea or land.
>
> With five small fishes and two loaves of bread,
> Large hungry crowds Jesus liberally fed.
> If you give tithes of all you have in store,
> He will shake, press down, and multiply more.

"That's true," Eliza thought, "sometimes I have so little at Kelton to give the children—a few dried cassavas, and some palm nuts they find in the jungle." She shook her head as if to clear her thoughts.

"They don't like palm nuts. I don't like palm nuts either, but at least it's something to eat when there's no money. And so far we haven't starved. It's like the loaves and the fishes—they weren't much, but nobody starved."

Eliza stumbled and caught herself with her walking stick to keep herself from sprawling headlong into the sand. "Where are those boys?" she thought. "They better come and help me. I must—keep—going. Mama always said, 'Don't quit. If you've got a job to do, don't quit.' Oh, Mama, what would you say if you knew I was walking 200 miles in Africa to get $200?" Then she chuckled to herself, "You always told me I'd do something special."

chapter four

After Slavery

Thinking of Mama brought back a flood of memories, for Eliza's mother had died just before Eliza returned to Africa this time, and her greatest source of encouragement and prayer backing was gone.

Eliza's mother, Jane Burdick, had been a very special person herself. Born a slave on the Burdick plantation in Bastrip County, Texas, in 1849, Jane had often told Eliza what it felt like to stand on the block to be sold.

"Liza, I was so scared . . . but God meant it to me for good, cause the Woodmores were so nice. And that's where I met your Papa."

Eliza could never hear the story often enough—how Mama had been sitting on the fence smoking her pipe when Papa came along. Doffing his faded blue work cap, Litt Davis had greeted her formally, "How do you do, Lady?"

And Jane, who was his elder by two years, haughtily replied, "How do you do, son?" But she couldn't resist his unabashed admiration and good humor, which made him one of the most popular young blades in the quarters. After a suitable courtship period, they "jumped the broom" and became man and wife. Eight years later the Emancipation Proclamation gave them their freedom.

Litt and Jane Davis had 11 children; Eliza was third. Jane was a praying woman who often spoke longingly of her "brothers and sisters" in Africa and told Eliza that when she was young she had dreamed of going to the continent of their forefathers. Eliza wrote in her autobiography, *My Call to Africa*, "I have always felt that her desire was transmitted to me—the desire to see Africa."

Her mother's prayers were part of Eliza's earliest memories. At the end of the long days in the cottonfields, Jane would drop to her knees beside the patchwork-covered bed and pray in a moaning tone which was almost melodic as her voice rose and fell with the rhythm of the words.

> O heavenly Father,
> This evening, Father, is the end of another long day.
> Oh, I thank You for keeping me through the day,
> And now here I am on my knees giving you praise.
> Bless the offspring of my dying body;
> Help me to raise them up in the way You'd have them go.

One day as Jane was working in the garden she heard Eliza's voice from behind the hedges at the bottom of the yard. Stepping closer to see to whom she was talking, she heard the lilting young voice, "O Lord, bless the offspring of my dying body . . . ."

"Liza, whatever are you doing?" Jane broke in. "Offspring is children—you ain't got no children!" But Eliza admitted that though she didn't know what it meant, the words had a beautiful sound to them.

Large families were an advantage for the sharecroppers. Litt Davis worked 100 acres of cotton, and Eliza and her two older brothers helped pick cotton when they were barely old enough to see over the tops of the popping bushes. Sometimes she stayed home to take care of sister Mary and baby Willy while Mama worked under the hot sun.

But with the best of crop and the biggest of families, Litt was always behind. Since he furnished his own food, implements, and horses, he received two-thirds of the profits from the sales. But it seemed there was always a huge bill waiting to be paid at the end of the summer, and he never had quite enough to pay it off.

One temptation for making extra money was gambling, and Litt Davis was a gambling man. Night after night he and the other men from the quarters played cards, hoping to win from each other what they had lost the night before.

One night Litt struck it rich—he had a winning streak that sent him home walking on air. Oh, how Jane would thank him now! He would drop the $100 with a flourish into her lap: "It's all yours, Janie. We can pay our debt to Mr. Woodmore, you can buy yourself a new dress, and there's enough for shoes for all the children," he would say proudly.

But it didn't happen quite that way. Jane was mending socks, sitting near the lamp to get all the benefit from its soft light. When he dropped the bills onto her ample lap, she looked up in disgust.

"Litt Davis, I don't need the Devil's money," she said, and she flung it through the open window beside her. Litt backed off speechless, unable to comprehend that she wouldn't accept his gift, no matter what the source. That night Litt sneaked away into the darkness and didn't return until morning.

But things were to change. One day when Eliza was seven years old, "Miss Ann," wife of the plantation owner, asked Litt to drive the buggy to a nearby town. She wanted to hear the famous singing evangelist, Ira Sankey, who was in the area.

Arriving at the meeting house, Litt parked the buggy near the side of the building, where he would be shaded from the sun while he waited for "Miss Ann."

Those were the days when black people didn't enter white folks' houses!

But on this hot afternoon all the windows of the church were open, and Sankey's voice easily carried out across the sleepy churchyard. Try as he might, Litt could not sleep; flies buzzed incessantly around the sweating horse and its driver. He would not help overhearing Sankey's message driving home his text: "The wages of sin is death . . . but the gift of God is eternal life." The voice rose higher as Sankey warmed up to his subject. "I dare say some of you fathers here are gambling men. Your wife is probably home right now praying for you."

Litt was growing angry under the sound of that penetrating message. Surely it was directed right at him, he told himself. "Miss Ann brought me here for a purpose; Jane must have been telling her about my gambling."

On the ride home, he replied to Mrs. Woodmore's enthusiastic report of "dear Brother Sankey's" message with monosyllabic grunts. He wasn't going to let on he'd heard a thing!

The next night Jane attended her usual weekly meeting at the nearby Baptist church. Litt had been going with her, more or less as a peace offering. But he began to suspect a conspiracy when Rev. Walker spoke on the very same text as Sankey had the day before, warning the drunkards and gamblers in the audience of their doom.

Litt was furious! Heads turned as he grumbled to Jane, "I'm not standing for this. You told that preacher about me, and I'm not listening to any more!"

Horrified, Jane saw him get up to leave the meeting. By now everyone in the congregation had turned around to see what was happening.

Eliza could tell the story as though she'd seen it all herself. "Papa just fell down hollering, and he couldn't help himself. 'Lord, have mercy!' he cried. He said if the Lord would let him get up, he would never do such a thing again.

"He got up and stumbled out of the church into the graveyard. He fell down again, and stayed there all night next to the grave of a man he used to gamble with. When Papa got up, he got up born-again Litt."

From that time until his death, in 1947, Litt Davis was a faithful deacon of the Baptist church, and a powerful preacher. People used to say he preached like Paul.

Litt's conversion was so dramatic that many others in the small black community also repented. Eliza loved to tell of Mr. Tippler Henry, who had also been gambling with her father. Someone told him of Litt's conversion while they were sitting around the card table. Tippler jumped up crying, "You tell me that Litt is converted?" And Eliza added triumphantly, "He was converted right there!"

As Eliza grew older she appreciated her father's discernment. One day a fiery evangelist came to town to preach, but Eliza just didn't feel right about him. Walking out to the field with her father one morning, she asked him what this preacher was doing. Litt replied gravely, "He ain't doing nothin'. He's just trying to get a feeling with these women around here. Maybe have a child." And that's what he did!

Litt was not an educated man, for slavery had succeeded well in keeping most black men out of school. But somewhere he had learned to read a little, and he could quote the Bible at length and tell you where the passage was found, too!

The Davises encouraged their children to go to school whenever they could be spared from the farm work. The dilapidated little schoolhouse opened only during a few months in the winter, but the children grandly referred to their teacher as "Professor Lawyer Taylor."

Eliza recalls that she was not good at all in math, but "Papa would help us. He would say, 'Liza, if a bale of cotton weighs

655 pounds and is selling at 11½ cents a pound, how much would it cost?' While we were getting out our pencils, father figured it all out."

Jane longed that her children would be educated, and she inspired Eliza to aim at becoming a teacher. She would tell her, "Liza, you're going to do something special one day." In later years Eliza would teach her own mother how to read and write.

It was soon evident that Eliza Davis was somebody who was going someplace. Her leadership ability didn't always take her in the right direction, however. One day reports came back to Teacher Taylor that some of the children had been stealing plums on the way home from school. The next morning Eliza arrived in the classroom to see blazoned across the blackboard these accusing words: "Plum Thieves, Eliza Davis, chairman."

But Eliza's heart had been softened by the gospel which her parents lived. And she loved to attend the lively worship services at the Baptist church.

There weren't many copies of "Old 800" in the church, so most people learned all verses of the hymns by memory. When they sang, they sang from the heart, swaying their bodies and clapping their hands with joy.

> Go preach my gospel, saith the Lord;
> Let this whole earth my grace receive . . . .
> He shall be saved who trusts the Lord,
> And he condemned who will not believe.

Sometimes Liza would sit up on the hill overlooking the river, watching the baptismal services below. She wanted to go down and be baptized "so bad," but she didn't yet fully understand why.

When she was 16 the pastor of the Baptist church, Elder Martin Hurd, approached her one day. "Eliza, you've been coming to church every Sunday, hearing the preaching of the Word of God. Don't you think you could trust the Lord as your personal Savior?"

Eliza's clear brown eyes looked right back into his. "Yes, Brother Hurd, if I believe on Him, I know He'll save me."

But it wasn't until the next series of "revival meetings" that Eliza moved forward to the "mourners' bench," where those under conviction would stay until they made their decision. Eliza recalled, "I went to the mourners' bench the first night and began to tremble. I stayed on it for about five nights during the special meeting.

"Then Mr. Hurd delivered a sermon on John 3:16, one I shall never forget. It answered my heart, and I accepted the Lord—and never felt so happy in my life. Immediately there seemed to be in my thoughts a longing to do something for Him, but what that 'something' was I did not know."

That "something" set Eliza apart when it came to the young men, who were more and more the center of her girlfriends' conversations. Giggling and whispering, the girls told about furtive love notes and "accidental" meetings on the way to school.

Eliza held herself aloof, and the boys soon caught on. When a new boy would be introduced to the Davis girls after church on a Sunday morning, the conversation would usually end up like this: "Mr. Henry Jones, this is Miss Mary Davis, and this is her sister, Miss Eliza Davis. *She* is a senior." And Eliza's cool "how-do-you-do" seemed to imply, "Don't get too close; there's no way you're going to talk me into love and marrying without knowing what I'm doing. I have something *special* to do."

But Eliza met her match in Phil, who had somehow twisted her heart around his finger with his suave words and worldly-wise ways. Walking home from church through the freshly mown fields, with the grasshoppers jumping up as they kicked the little piles of remaining hay aside, "Phil asked, 'Will you go to the ice cream social with me on Saturday night? There's nobody else I'd like to take as much as you, Miss Davis!'"

It took all her control for Eliza to say, "Thank you, Mr. Phil, but I will have to ask my parents." As soon as Phil turned off the lane toward his farm, Eliza flew home, her long legs skimming over the grounds as they used to when she was chosen the best ballplayer in the school.

Kneading bread dough in the hot, sun-filled kitchen, Mama listened to Eliza's request in silence. Then she said thoughtfully, "Child, you can go if Papa agrees. But, Eliza, if you're goin' to go to college, go to college. Don't have no truck with a boy like Phil."

Hardly daunted, Eliza changed her school clothes and saddled her mother's horse, Seelom. The horse seemed to sense her jubilation and needed little urging to cover the miles to her friend Mary's home so she could tell her the exciting news.

But Mary seemed to be bursting with her own news, and as soon as the girls could slip away to their favorite hideaway in the orchard, Mary burst out, "Oh Eliza, I'm so happy. Phil was here last night, and he told me that he loves me!"

A heartbroken Eliza rode back home, suffering her first pains of unrequited love, too willful to accept her defeat. Stopping to mull over the situation, she heard the mournful call of a dove perched in the lower branches of a tree along the road. "He sounds like I feel," complained Eliza. Then she closed her eyes and in her strong young voice spoke out, "Lord, if it's your will that I marry Phil, I want that dove to fly from that tree when I open my eyes."

In later years she would laughingly recall, "That dove wouldn't fly. I got so mad I picked up a rock and threw it at it."

The next afternoon Eliza was "flat-breaking" some land that Mama wanted dug up for planting turnips. Eliza was glad to get out of the house to plod slowly through the moist-smelling sod behind Paul, one of her father's four mules. It gave her time to think, but the more she thought about Phil, the madder she got. Suddenly she burst out loud, "How could Phil do this to me?" only to see her mother coming across the field toward her. Not wanting her mother to know how upset she was, she began singing, "There is a fountain Phil-led with blood." Mama never did catch on!

Later that evening Papa came to Eliza saying that Mama had told him she wanted to go to the social with Phil. "I didn't want to tell you this, Honey, but Phil has already been married. He married a very nice girl, Mr. Mouton's daughter. She has two children. And he quit her, just like that. Carol is one of the sweetest girls you'd want to meet. And if he gets you, he'll quit you too."

Eliza just squeezed Papa's arm, but she didn't tell him he'd already done just that.

Eliza would have other proposals, more serious in intent, in the next years, but let a suitor make his declaration, and Eliza would quickly make hers: she didn't want "to get her mind confused." She knew there was something special that God wanted her to do.

chapter five

The Year 1900

The year 1900 was a dark memory to the Davis family. Boll weevils destroyed their entire cotton crop.

Papa had gone off looking for a job, and the family hadn't heard from him for weeks. Paul, Betty, Luke, and Bill—their four faithful mules—had been mortgaged, and Seelom had been sold.

Eliza had hoped that her earnings for picking cotton would pay her school fees for the next year. At 50 cents a hundred pounds, she could save a good bit of the $38 she needed for the year.

But now the crop was gone and Papa was gone, and it seemed that all hope of going back to Guadalupe College was gone.

At age 20, Eliza had spent one year at the teachers' training college, 40 miles from home. She had just loved it—everything but math!

Going off to teachers' training college sounds so matter-of-fact today, but for a black girl in the South at the turn of the century, it was a miracle. With slavery dead only 35 years, few black children aspired to even a high-school education, and much fewer were given the opportunity. Southern whites scoffed at "Negroes" who got an education and then wouldn't labor in the fields.

Eliza had worked hard, and the family had sacrificed to pay the fees. In the Bible classes and devotional sessions she had matured and was beginning to get some idea of what God might want her to do. During a chapel service Rev. H. Bouey, who had just returned from Liberia, challenged the student body to missionary service. Eliza was one of the three students who had responded to the invitation for volunteer missionary service.

And the seed of a plan was sown in her breast. But now she had lost all hope!

One morning toward the end of that devastating summer, Eliza borrowed a horse to ride to town to get a few necessities for the family. Hoping there might be a letter from Papa, she stopped to ask for mail at the post office.

To her surprise the postmistress handed her a letter addressed to her from Guadalupe College. Tearing it open, she could hardly believe her eyes as she read: "Dear Miss Eliza, 'Trust in the Lord and do good; so shalt thou dwell in the land. In all thy ways acknowledge Him, and He shall direct thy paths.' We heard that the boll weevils destroyed your parents' cotton crop, so special arrangements have been made for you to enter college this year. Come at once!"

When Eliza returned to Guadalupe she found that the "special arrangements" included a part-time job in the school kitchen. Every evening she mixed dough for the next day's bread in a huge tub and let it set in the warm kitchen overnight. At 4:30 the next morning she was up baking.

But between the little she earned in the kitchen and the egg money that Mama sent, she managed. She recalled, "Mama used to send me 10 cents in an envelope . . . we used to get 10 cents a dozen for eggs. I would get change and take out 1 cent for a tithe."

In the spring of 1901 Eliza received a phone call from her brother-in-law in Bastrop.

As she flew down the hall to take the call in the president's office, her mind conjured up a thousand cries. "Is it Papa? Has he been hurt? Or is Mama sick?"

Grabbing the phone, Eliza heard, "You've got to come home. Willie took a fit and fell into the fire. The doctor says he's dyin'."

Standing at the bedside of her dying brother, Eliza could see that her mother had reached the breaking point. Her father was still not home, though word had come that he was trying to find a place for the family to live in Taylor. Slipping quietly out of the sickroom, Eliza went to the well-used, carved oak pump organ that was the family's prize possession, and began pumping vigorously. "Ask the Savior to help you; He will comfort and bless you, He will carry you through."

Willy died.

At the funeral, in Antioch, Uncle Ike, the licensed preacher, allowed Eliza to say a few words for the family.

"I was at school when the message came. I got home to find Mama tryin' to keep a big heart. Papa has mortgaged everything we have—we ain't got nothin' at all now. Looks like everything has gone against us, but Jesus has promised never to leave us alone."

Watching Mama in the front row, Eliza saw the sagging shoulders straighten with resolve, and she would tell people later, "Mama got happy and never did cry."

On the way home from the funeral, Eliza broached the subject of her going back to school.

"Mama, I've decided to stay home and help you. When Papa gets a job and things are better, I can go back again. But for now, you need me at home."

Her mother wouldn't hear of it. "No, no, Eliza, you must go back. When I'm dead and buried and my bones are bleached in the earth, you'll have need of this training. God will carry us through this trouble too."

Eliza completed her second year at Guadalupe, earning a teacher's diploma. Since there were so few trained black teachers, teachers' training colleges used the system of having senior students teach younger children while completing their own courses.

Eliza was able to get a job teaching lower grades in Waco, Texas, while she worked toward her teacher's certificate at Central Texas College. Things had improved at home too, with her father getting a job and purchasing a house for the family in Taylor, Texas.

After completing her academic course at Central Texas College, Eliza was asked to serve on the faculty; she taught for five years and then served as matron.

On February 2, 1911, the faculty and students gathered for their usual morning devotional hour. As the students filed in they saw that Professor Hill would be leading the devotion, and Eliza overheard one of the boys say to his friend, "Here we go, all the way around the world and halfway back again."

While Rev. Hill prayed for India, China, Japan, and Africa, Eliza's heart was suddenly filled with an overwhelming desire to see her brothers and sisters in Africa. It seemed as though her soul swelled out and grew so that her body was a tiny little core of her real self that seemed to reach heaven. As clearly as if she were there, she saw black people from Africa passing before the judgment seat of Christ, weeping and moaning, "But no one ever told us You died for us."

Eliza sat in her seat long after the students had fled out of the chapel, released from their unwilling captivity. When she finally got up to go back to her office she met the school president, Dr. John Strong, who noticed her unusually pensive behavior.

Touching her elbow to slow her down, he asked with concern, "Are you all right, Miss Davis?"

Without thinking Eliza blurted out, "I'm fine, Dr. Strong. I'm going to Africa."

"Oh, please, Miss Davis, don't let yourself get carried away by that foolishness," he remonstrated. "You don't have to go over there to be a missionary—we have enough Africa over here!"

Two years later Eliza sat at her desk, her back straight and unbending, even after ten hours a day on her feet. A matron's job included many things—cleaning up the toilets after the girls, checking dirty linens, ordering groceries. It seemed she ran all day long, with never a minute to catch her breath.

But this letter had to be written—and written carefully.

She started again, "Dear Dr. Strong and members of the Board of Trustees of Central Texas College . . . ."

She had composed the letter so often in her mind as she rushed from one task to another during the day that it should come easily. But resignations were never easy to write, especially this one. Eliza knew that the faculty thought her idea of going to Africa was crazy. More than one had told her so.

It was now two years since God had spoken to her so clearly in that morning chapel; and though she had told Dr. Strong most emphatically that she was going, practically speaking it had been out of the question at the time.

There were still six brothers and sisters younger than she at home (Mary had died just a few years after Willy), and she had been helping Jenny Belle, Ellen, and Vic through school. But now there were others in the family who could help Papa, and the time had come when she could begin to fulfill her own God-given ambition.

She began again:

Dear Dr. Strong:

It is with deep regret that I find it necessary to tender my resignation as matron of Central Texas College. God has called me to serve my brethren in Africa, and I can no longer refuse. Please accept my resignation as of the end of the school year.

Sincerely, Eliza L. Davis

The Year 1900   35

What had seemed a simple matter turned into a furor. The board members certainly did not agree that Miss Davis should go to Africa as a missionary. They reminded her that the Negro in America was far worse off than his African brothers, and that the battle for equality and education had just begun. And they needed her at the college—she was the best fundraiser they had.

Though sweetly refuting their arguments, Eliza found herself seething inside. "They just want me to keep cleaning the toilets and picking up after everyone because no one else wants to do it."

But in all fairness, she realized that a black woman had never gone out as a missionary from Texas before, and the leaders of the Baptist Convention did not believe she was able to take on such a pioneering work.

The president of the state convention came to speak with Eliza personally about her request. When he saw her stubborn determination, he told her he thought she was losing her mind.

"Miss Davis," he reprimanded sternly, "you don't have the money, and we ministers stand between you and the people to keep you from getting the money!"

Eliza did not answer him, but deep down her heart responded, "But you don't stand between me and my God!"

After weeks of arguments and discussions, the board agreed to call a special meeting at which Eliza could personally present her reasons for her decision. She spent sleepless nights working out her speech, writing and rewriting, until she had it word-perfect.

At the same time, in her devotions God gave her a poem which expressed her longing to go to Africa. Its message unfolded like a flower, gripping her own heart and reinforcing her conviction that she was making the right decision. Whether the board agreed or not, she was determined to leave Central Texas College and begin her preparations. Somewhere, somehow God would provide what she needed to get to Africa.

Eliza dressed carefully for the board meeting. She was always neat and precise, but this afternoon her white blouse with the dozen tiny pearl buttons down the front was starched immaculately, her blue paisley tie was tied as carefully as any man's, and her high-button shoes glistened.

There was no sign of nervousness or deference as she stood up to present her case before the board. She read defiance in the eyes of some of the men before her, and a faintly bemused curiosity in others.

Breathing an inward prayer for help, Eliza began.

"Gentlemen, led by the Spirit of God, I have found my life's work. I believe God would have me go to Africa to take the gospel of salvation to the people in darkness...."

As Eliza outlined her reasons for going, the men lost some of their defiant demeanor, listening intently to every word this slip of a girl was saying.

"Not only is the Holy Spirit calling me, but those are my brothers and sisters—your brothers and sisters. While we Negroes were brought here to America, seemingly for our harm, God has used it for some good. We have come to know Jesus Christ and are no longer bound in chains of witchcraft and heathenism. Just as Moses returned to his own people after he had learned the wisdom of the Egyptians, so I believe God wants me to go back and share with my lost brethren the education he has privileged me to get in America ...

"I believe my life's work is not in America, but Africa, and that's where I *must* go...."

"In closing, I would like to recite a poem which God has led me to write in these past weeks as I've been struggling with my decision.

> My African brother is calling me;
> Hark! Hark! I hear his voice.
> In a land more dense with work I see
> That work is now my choice."

Glancing straight into the eyes of her most vocal antagonist, Eliza went on:

> "Would you say 'stay' when God said 'go'
> To that dark foreign land and
> Spread the light? Would you say 'no'
> That bright their souls might stand?
> There he bows down to wood and stone—
> He thinks his way is right.
> And when from earth his soul has gone,
> To hell he takes his flight."

As Eliza's clear, strong voice rang out, carried away by

her own sense of the dramatic, the men shifted uneasily in their chairs.

> "Christ on His throne could've been at ease
> When all the world was lost,
> But gave His life for death to please;
> His lifeblood paid the cost.
>
> My African brother awaits my call;
> The Lord bids me now depart.
> His word is firm and cannot fail;
> I'll trust His Word and start.
>
> Kindred and friends, I bid farewell—
> I'm going on yonder shore.
> The Word of God is mine to tell;
> My brother is my store.
>
> I'll work for him with all my might,
> And try his heart to reach.
> I'll work till age shall dim my sight;
> I'll to him God's Word teach.
>
> I'll look to God to guide my way
> And trust His promise sure;
> And since He leads I will not stray—
> His Word is so secure.
>
> And when on earth my time shall come
> To stand before the King,
> I'll see in Christ I did win some,
> I'll hear my brothers sing."

Eliza sat down, realizing that she had never once even looked at the notes clenched in her hand. Then, startled, she heard the board members applauding. Dr. Strong stood up, cleared his throat to bring the members to attention, looked at Eliza, and said:

"Miss Davis, your eloquence and sincerity have moved us deeply. I for one can no longer stand in the way of your fulfilling your life's ambition.

"I can sense that the rest of the members of the board feel as I do. We are not able to provide the necessary funds for your venture—you will have to trust God for that. But we can release you from further obligations to Central Texas College and assure you of our prayers."

Before Eliza finished the school year at Central, she met the man who was to be her friend and helper: Rev. James Kelly, the corresponding secretary of the Foreign Missions Board of the General Baptist Convention of Texas. As a part of the National Baptist Convention, the Texas group was responsible for any missionaries going out from Texas, and so Eliza came to Rev. Kelly's attention.

In the months that followed, Rev. Kelly took Eliza to black churches in Houston, New Orleans, and other places and helped raise support for her. One church gave her a Singer sewing machine to take with her.

Word finally came from Dr. Jordan of the National Baptist Convention that she would be working with Miss Susie Taylor in Fortesville, Liberia. A ship would be leaving from New York for Liverpool on December 12, 1913, and he would accompany her to New York.

Eliza never spoke of the farewells with her family in Texas. But one can imagine the mingled pride, joy, and sorrow as she kissed Mama and Papa goodbye, hugged her sisters and brothes, and tried not to look at Mama's tears and Papa's anguish as they stood in the doorway of the little clapboard house, watching her ride away. Liberia was a never-never land they could barely find on a map, and it would be seven years before they could see Eliza again.

In New York, Eliza and Dr. Jordan stayed in the home of another missionary to Liberia the night before the Celtic sailed. The following morning Dr. Jordan took Eliza to the docks and made sure that she was comfortably settled in her tiny cabin.

Standing at the rail as Dr. Jordan prepared to disembark, a terrifying thought suddenly struck Eliza. Putting her hand on his arm, she asked, "Dr. Jordan, how must I begin my work when I get to Africa?"

"Any way you can, my dear," was his reply as he turned and walked down the gangplank.

chapter six

The Love of Liberty

A sudden wave jolted Eliza out of her reverie. She had been so immersed in her thoughts that she had hardly noticed that the sky had suddenly turned dark and that the sea was now a sullen gray cauldron. Far up the beach the boys were scurrying for cover under the overhang of a huge boulder, but Eliza could not push herself to join them before the deluge fell.

Equatorial rainfalls, as nowhere else on earth, pour as if all the faucets of heaven were opened at once. In seconds Eliza was soaked to the skin, shivering in the suddenly chilling air. But she doggedly kept on moving up the beach, one foot ahead of the other, one step closer to Monrovia.

By Friday the little trio was moving at a snail's pace along the hot sand. Robert and Tussnah's feet, ordinarily toughened from going barefoot all their lives, were now burned and blistered. Walking in the surf relieved the heat, but the salt irritated the raw blisters so that they could only stay in the water for a short time.

Tussnah took to walking on the sides of his feet, so that Mother Eliza couldn't help teasing him, "You look like a bowlegged cowboy from Texas."

By now the boys were no longer scampering ahead playing in the sand, but rather Mother had to urge them along to keep up with her. "This is Friday, children; we should be there tomorrow night, or the latest on Sunday. But we must keep going so we can catch the steamer back to Greenville on Monday morning."

The thought of the steamer put new life into the boys for a few minutes, but they were soon complaining about their feet and how tired they were.

Mother had an unusual gift of story-telling, and had been able to amuse and capture the hearts of children all her life. So once again she put her own aches and discomforts behind her and tried to take the boys' minds off their troubles.

But even Eliza's usual dramatic story-telling failed to hold the boys' interest, and before long they were lagging behind, and she was left to her own thoughts.

She remembered her first contact with the tribal people had given Susie Taylor and herself a clear indication of what God wanted them to do in Liberia. The natives in the interior villages were to be their mission field, though first they had to convince the Liberian Baptist convention, with whom the National Baptists cooperated in their work in Liberia. Mission work among primarily tribal people was rare in those days, and particularly for women it was a dangerous venture in the uncharted interior.

It had been a shock to Eliza when she had realized that Liberia was still divided into two distinct population groups—the Americo-Liberians and the tribal people. But even in the first few days in Monrovia she had discovered that the descendants of the first colonists carried a veneer of sophistication—a pride of heritage that confined their social contacts and political efforts to their own group.

Eliza had read every Liberian history book she could find, and she remembered how the country had been founded. In the early nineteenth century many American whites had been restless about the slave situation. The American Colonization Society was formed to find a place in Africa where freed slaves could be returned to develop their own country. Others who backed the project had less-pure motives: many slave owners felt that the presence of large numbers of freed slaves would disturb the contentment of their own slaves.

The first contingent of freed slaves left the U.S.A. in the spring of 1820 and settled on Cape Montserrado, the site of present-day Monrovia. Of the 86 original settlers, 49 died within six months. The area was a hellhole of disease, with malaria, yellow fever, and dysentery running rampant. There was no doctor in the colony.

Settlers negotiated with tribal chiefs to purchase an area 140 miles long and 40 miles wide along the coast. The payment for the initial settlement of 30 huts included muskets, powder, basins, knives, walking sticks, hats, and shoes and was valued at less than $75.

But the native tribes were suspicious of the colonists. The population of Liberia had been decimated by two centuries of slaving, and the tribes believed that the colonists were simply a camouflage for renewed slave trading. They prepared to attack.

Jehudi Ashmun, the second supervisor of the colony, began training the settlers to defend themselves. Though by now over 4000 colonists had arrived, within a short time more than 2100 had died from disease.

When the attack came, women fought alongside their men against natives armed with spears and battle axes. A lone cannon gave the beleaguered colonists an advantage.

Ashmun, one of the few white leaders Liberia had, threw his lot in with the freed slaves and did much to establish the colony. At one time he denied all "drones" the privilege of drawing rations from the central storehouse, in order to enlist their cooperation.

It was difficult for those liberated slaves who had known the horrors and degradation of slavery to now suddenly become industrious and productive workers for the new nation. Rather, they assumed the veneer of sophistication and pride which they had seen in their own Southern masters in the U.S.

The colonists struggled to maintain the traditions which they had brought with them from America. A social gathering became an occasion for formal dark suits, top hats, and long satin gowns. Their houses were an attempt at Southern architecture, though with few materials and limited skills they lacked perfection, and many were never completed, giving the appearance of houses gutted by fire.

The Colonization Society provided no funds for development other than to continue to dump untrained and impoverished settlers on its shores. There was a pathos about the stunted settlement with its follies on the rocky hillside, and a people planted down without money or home on a coast of yellow fever and malaria to make what they could of an Africa from which their families were torn centuries before.

Yet, motivated by their motto, "The love of liberty brought us here," they struggled to develop a new country out of the primitive and hostile environment. The colonists became masters at diplomacy. The republic which was born in 1847 became the first independent nation in Africa. Beginning with its first president, Joseph Jenkins Roberts, it was ruled by a succession of able statesmen and stable governments until 1980, when President Tolbert was assassinated in a coup d'etat.

Gradually the tribal people became attracted to the jobs and things available in Monrovia and became the willing servants of their colonial masters.

But the most serious internal problem continued to be the relationship of the Americo-Liberians, as the settlers were called, and the 16 major tribes of Liberia, who made up 90 percent of the population. The 1847 constitution, based on the American document, granted citizenship only to blacks, but limited the franchise to those who owned property. The trappings of civilization, such as Western clothing, use of English, and Southern architecture, all became synonymous with the Americo-Liberian's way of life. It was a charade of royalty.

Christianity became synonymous with civilization as well, and the settlers gave the impression that speaking English was a prerequisite to becoming a Christian.

The founding fathers had come with a twin purpose: to snuff out slavery at its source, and to bring Christianity to Africa. The first settlers formed a church on board ship, and the Providence Baptist Church in Monrovia is the oldest permanent building in the country and the oldest Baptist church on the continent.

Christianity became a facade for civilization; the settlers were great churchgoers. Many of the fledging nation's early leaders were devout and earnest Christians, but others used the church for their own social ends, living lives of immorality outside. The Liberian church historian, Conrad Wold, would write many years later, "The strategy of early missionaries was to use the colonists as stepping stones to evangelization of tribes. But they never got past the stepping stones."

Thus when Eliza had first arrived in Liberia, she found well-attended churches in all the "civilized" towns she visited, with both the Baptist and Methodist denominations strong. Happily, whereas in the past missionaries and pastors had been discouraged from taking civilizing Christianity to the "naturally ignorant natives," attitudes were beginning to change. Though she and Susie Taylor faced resistance, they were finally granted permission to open a school for native children several miles in the interior from Fortesville.

Eliza could still visualize the happy group of children heading out of Fortesville to the new mission school. Each one had carried a box or basin on his head, with some children almost hidden under their load. Eliza still laughed to herself as she remembered how they had argued among themselves for the privilege of carrying the shiny new washtub, which had been a gift from one of the ladies in the church.

For months Eliza and Susie Taylor had spent every minute they could spare from their teaching responsibilities to plan and prepare for the new mission. They decided to call it the Bible Industrial Academy, signifying the double aim the school would have: teaching the children to read the Bible, and teaching them to farm and do other tasks that would make them more productive people.

Mr. Reeves had been a great help in purchasing lumber and hiring natives to build the house on the site. Every inch of ground had to be cleared of centuries of heavy growth, and only a small section of the large track was cleared initially.

To Eliza the two-room hut was beautiful. She and Susie had supervised the men as they cut saplings and built a mud house on a bamboo frame, covering it with palm thatch. The dirt floor was pounded and smoothed and covered with mats. The two windows had no need of glass, but she had shown the workers how to make wooden shutters which could be closed when the torrential rains beat against the house. Until another hut could be built, the little boys would be staying with them.

In the months that followed, the women had more land cleared for farming. Neither had ever made a Liberian farm before, but the native workers helped them, slashing the undergrowth with fierce-looking cutlasses and burning the brush to clear several acres of land at a time. How Eliza would have loved to have the faithful plodding mules from poppa's farm! But instead she doggedly hoed the fertile-looking soil, working long hours with the boys as she planted indigenous cassava and roots, such as edoes and even coffee scions.

During their first year at BIA, Susie and Eliza divided their responsibilities. Susie taught the small group of boys in a makeshift shelter every morning and then supervised their work in the gardens. Eliza traveled up and down the rivers and creeks by canoe, visiting the villages upstream. Taking Jude, an interpreter, with her, she would tell the people about Jesus, who died for them. She would encourage the parents to send their children to the mission to be taught.

Gradually the number of boys increased. The children arrived naked or with a scanty loincloth wrapped around them, and

Susie and Eliza would dig out a shirt or make a pair of shorts from the few boxes of clothes they had brought with them.

The villagers were friendly people who welcomed this "God-woman" and extended their simple hospitality to Eliza whenever she passed through. Though she had to speak with an interpreter, she soon knew many of the villagers by name, asking about their children and giving advice about their ailments. She never passed by without stopping to pray with those who gathered around her, and frequently had the joy of leading some of these people to the Lord.

But even though Eliza experienced warmth and acceptance from many of the villagers, she was horrified at some of the practices she encountered.

The first time she saw a mother force hot pepper down her baby's throat, almost strangling the screaming infant, she had to stop herself from grabbing the baby from the mother's arms.

"What are they doing to that baby?" she demanded.

Jude patiently explained, "They must begin giving the child 'man's food' a few days after it is born or it will not grow up to be strong and healthy. If the child drinks only mother's milk, it will remain weak."

Jude was a great help in explaining the many different customs which disturbed Eliza as she went deeper into the jungle. She grew accustomed to seeing infants being washed in water so hot she could barely stand to touch it herself, or to see their squirming bodies being rubbed with a white, pasty mixture so that they looked like miniature clowns.

"That's to keep the devils away," explained Jude.

"What's the scar on the girl's arm?" she asked one day as she came across a young girl folding her arms across her budding breasts as she stopped to take a rest from grinding palm nuts.

"Those are scars from the bracelets she wore as an infant; they prove that her parents put jewelry on her as a baby."

Eliza shuddered to think of the painful sores which developed as the bracelets grew too tight around the growing young arm.

But what distressed Eliza most was that the little girls represented an article of trade to their parents. One father replied to her persistent request to send his girl to the mission, "We don't give girls away; we sell them."

Tribal girls were betrothed at about seven years of age—sometimes to men many years older than they, who already had several wives. At the age of 10 or 12 they were taken to live with the man's people to learn "his fashion."

Since the dowry was paid when the arrangement was concluded, it was a waste of time and effort to educate a girl who already belonged to some other family. It was better to utilize her services in the hut and garden as long as she was at home.

Eliza and Susie had just about given up hoping that they would ever be able to have a tribal girl at the mission.

One morning a distraught young woman from Fortesville arrived at BIA. She had a round-faced little girl of about three years tied on her hip, held by a hand-woven cloth in typical tribal fashion. Asking for Eliza, words tumbled over themselves so that Eliza barely understood her Liberian English.

"Dis girl's mama, she goin' to kill me. She goin' to take the baby. Her papa give her to me so dat she get schoolin', but her mama don't like dat."

Calming the distraught woman down, Eliza began to piece the story together.

Angeline, the young woman, lived in Fortesville. A Bassa man had come into the town to work for her uncle and began to appreciate the benefits of civilization. After a few months on the job, he went back to his village in the hinterland, returning with his daughter.

He brought the child to Angeline, since he knew she believed in helping native children, and he asked her to bring his daughter up. Angeline took the little girl, giving her the "civilized" name of Maude in place of her tribal name. She found the little one quick to learn, as well as obedient.

Several weeks after Maude was brought to Angeline her mother arrived at the door, demanding her child back. Angeline refused and quickly sent word to Maude's father about what had happened. The father was insistent that Maude stay in town to be reared in a civilized manner.

That night Maude's mother broke into the bedroom and took the little girl away, disappearing into the night before Angeline realized what had happened.

As soon as the father could get away from the job, he went home to retrieve Maude. But he warned Angeline that his wife's people were angry and threatened to steal the child again, even if they had to poison Angeline to do so.

With this fear driving her, Angeline came to Eliza to plead that she take Maude and bring her up as her father wished.

Eliza took the little girl in her arms, certain that God had answered her prayer and that Maude was just the first of many girls she would rescue from a hopeless future. So confident was she in her own lofty purposes that the mother's anguish never entered her mind.

By the end of the year 1915 Susie and Eliza were well-established in their ministry at BIA. The harvest from their little farm produced enough to stave off hunger for a time, the children were learning well, and several hundred villagers had accepted Christ.

Eliza was confident that she had indeed found her life's work. Letters from home were infrequent but longed for, and when news came that the steamer had stopped in Buchanan, Eliza waited impatiently for the mail to be brought to the mission.

Included in the letters from her family and friends was a letter from Rev. James Kelly.

Sinking to the ground, Eliza read with dismay that the Baptist Convention of Texas had split from the National Baptists. Since Eliza was the only missionary from Texas, she would have to be replaced by missionaries under the National Baptists. Eliza's infant lifework had just heard its death knell!

Eliza did the only thing she knew to do—she prayed. Many nights long after Susie was asleep under her mosquito netting, Eliza knelt beside her cot, her head buried in Mama's colorful patchwork quilt. Bewildered, disappointed, alone, she poured out her heart to her Father.

> O Lord, You sent me here; You told me this was my life's work. The leaders of the convention have told me I must get ready to come home. But Father, I am not under their orders; I'm under Yours, and I won't leave until You tell me to go.

For many months there was no further word from the mission. Each time the steamer brought mail from America, she would hastily glance through the letters, almost fearful of seeing another from the Convention, yet longing for the suspense to be broken.

As the months stretched on, Eliza and Susie tried to put the ominous news behind them. God was blessing their little mission. They now had 50 children in the school, including several little girls. A two-story, bamboo-and-thatch building, 36 by 40 feet, was complete, and the boys were living on the top floor, while the ground floor served as a classroom and dining room.

Even more thrilling to Eliza was the response to the gospel among the tribal people. Within the year more than a thousand converts had accepted Christ in the villages.

Toward the end of 1916 Eliza visited a village far upstream, where she had never been before, and was away a week. It was an exciting time, though Eliza's heart was moved as she saw little children ill with fever, with no medical care available. On this trip she arrived in one village to find the women all gathered in a hut with a woman in a difficult delivery. Though Eliza had little experience and no training, the women begged her to help, but it was too late. The exhausted young mother died in agony, and her infant with her. Eliza would never forget the wailing and the "talking" drums that throbbed through the night as her soul went back to her ancestors.

After a week in the interior, Eliza had returned to the mission in a downpour. The boys reached the dugout canoe on the sandy bottom and jumped out to tug it up on the shore.

The roar of the rain, falling like great waterfalls over the edge of the clouds, muted their voices so that Eliza couldn't hear what they were saying. They steadied the canoe as she stepped out into the water, her drenched skirt clinging to her thighs and trailing in the fast-moving current.

Eliza was so thoroughly soaked that she involuntarily shivered as she waded to shore, carrying her sodden canvas bag of equally sodden clothes. It seemed as though she had been wet for a week, though the storm only broke in the night while she was sleeping in one of the villager's huts.

Shouting over the storm, Eliza directed the boys to take the cassavas she had bought from the natives back to their house. Clutching her Bible (wrapped in oilcloth under her arm) and carrying her shapeless, mud-plastered shoes in the other hand, Eliza trudged up the trail to her own thatched hut, looking forward to getting out of her wet clothes.

She half-expected to see Susie standing in the doorway. She usually had a good meal prepared for her when she came back from her trips into the hinterland.

But there was no sign of life in the room as she pushed open the door. The heavy clouds cast a gloomy gray spell over everything, and the shutters on the rainward side had been closed to keep out some of the water that insisted on running down the frame, making mud puddles on the floor below. A damp, musty smell permeated everything.

Growing accustomed to the dim light, Eliza saw Susie lying on her cot, several blankets piled on her and pulled over her head. "Not another malaria attack," groaned Eliza as she pushed the door shut.

"Susie, it's me, Eliza. What's the matter?"

A violent spasm shook the form huddled on the bed, and Susie's wan face emerged above the covers. "I'll be all right—I came down with the fever last night, but I've run out of quinine."

Stripping off her sodden clothes, Eliza thankfully put on a dry robe and slippers and toweled her springy black hair to shake out the moisture. How thankful she was once again for the kerosene stove so she didn't have to struggle with wet wood that sputtered and went out!

Susie was grateful for the hot tea and for the quinine Eliza fished out of her wet bag. "I'm going to Buchanan tomorrow to get supplies, so I'll get more," Eliza said consolingly.

Susie seemed to feel a bit better as she listened to Eliza's enthusiastic report of her trip, and even managed to laugh as Eliza told her how she had fallen out of the canoe when it hit a hidden log in the river.

"Those boys fished me out like a wet rag," and Eliza's infectious laughter filled the gloomy room.

"And what happened here at BIA while I was away?" she asked as she finished her story.

Susie recounted several problems: the boys had not been doing their work in the garden; they had run out of salt; and the workmen had come for their money, but she hadn't had enough to pay them.

"Oh, yes," she added almost as an afterthought; "we had a visitor yesterday afternoon. Mr. G. Thompson George, a man from some British country in South America, passed this way. He's just come to settle in Liberia and is visiting the Reeves' in Fortesville. I guess Mr. Reeves must have told him to see what we're doing here at the mission. He seemed very nice."

Asking a few more questions about the week's activities, Eliza could see that Susie was getting tired, so she urged her to go to sleep. For a long time she sat in the darkness next to her bed, praying about her growing concern for Susie's health. The malaria attacks were coming more frequently, and there was a gnawing fear that she would not be able to stay in Liberia much longer.

The torrential rain ceased as suddenly as it had begun, and the dripping of the water running off the thatched roof was the only sound in the night as Eliza crawled thankfully under Mama's patchwork quilt and fell asleep.

"I wonder if Susie felt like this when she was walking to Monrovia to catch the ship," Eliza heard herself saying aloud as she realized she had been lost in a reverie of more than 23 years earlier. She hadn't thought of Susie Taylor for a long time, but how vividly she now remembered the weeks of agonizing decision while Susie debated whether she could remain in Liberia.

Her body had been continually wracked with fever, and she had lost so much weight that she was too weak to work. It became obvious that God was not going to cure Susie of malaria and that she would have to leave the fever-infested country for safer climates.

With no steamers coming to Bassa because of World War I, Susie decided to walk more than 70 miles to Monrovia to catch a ship for the United States from there.

It still brought a lump to Eliza's throat when she remembered their tearful and final farewell. But then she straightened her sagging shoulders and called to Tussnah and Robert, "Hurry up. If Susie could do it sick with malaria, we'll make it to Monrovia too."

chapter seven

One Breath From Death

The heat on Saturday morning seemed more oppressive than ever to Eliza as she dragged her tired body along. To the boys' constant whining, "When we going to be there?" she could only say, "Soon, children, soon."

But from what the villagers with whom they stayed last night had told her, Monrovia was at least a day-and-a-half's walk further—that is, if they could keep up a normal pace.

Far ahead on the beach she could see a break in the sand, which could mean that the shoreline turned in around another bay, or it could mean yet another river. She had lost track of how many rivers and streams they had crossed; some were shallow enough to ford at low tide, and several times friendly fishermen had taken them across. But twice they had to swim against a heavy current, and she feared she did not have the strength for that again.

Getting closer, she was relieved to see that it was a wide but fairly shallow stream, and since it was low tide they should be able to cross it easily. Eliza had a special dread of snakes, but fortunately they weren't common in the salt water near the mouth of the river. More than once on her treks inland to villages she had felt a slimy body move past her as she crossed a murky jungle creek, but praise God, none had ever bitten her.

The boys seemed eager to get across and were already almost on the other side when Eliza stepped into the cool water. She had taken off her heavy boots and tied them to her belt so she wouldn't lose them should she slip on a slippery rock submerged under the surface.

Carefully she looked for flat surfaces on the rocks, feeling with her bare foot to get a firm footing. The current was swifter midstream than it had looked from the shore, but as long as the water was only up to her waist, she could maintain her balance.

About midstream, as Eliza began feeling for another solid place to put her weight, she realized that she had come to a dropoff where she could not touch bottom. "I guess I'll have to swim part of the way after all," she said to herself and threw herself into the water. Fortunately, the boys had taken her helmet and bag with them, so she wasn't encumbered with anything but the boots tied around her waist.

She could see a rock jutting out of the water just a few yards ahead of her, and she headed for that when suddenly she was drawn into an eddying whirlpool, her hands and feet flaying the water. A strong undertow caught her helpless body and drew her out to sea. The roar of the surf drowned out her cries.

As the waters closed over her head, she struggled to surface with a furious determination not to let the sea overpower her. "Father," she cried out, "don't let me die now; who will take care of all my children?"

Her lungs felt as though they were bursting when a swell lifted her long enough to draw in a great gulp of air before it dashed her down into the sea with unmitigated fury. She felt herself being drawn under with such force that her desperate attempts to force herself upward were as useless as holding back a giant boulder from tumbling down a hill.

"Mother . . . Mother . . . Mother."

Eliza could hear the voices of children calling her name from a far distance. As she turned over and opened her eyes, she saw Tussnah and Robert bending over her, tears streaming down their faces.

"Oh, Mother, are you all right?" cried Tussnah as he saw her eyes open. "We thought you were dead."

"We saw you being carried out to sea, and we tried to get back to help you, but the waves were too strong," Robert blurted out, hardly able to believe that Mother was still alive.

"Then a big wave picked you up and threw you back on the shore; we just pulled you away from the water so that you wouldn't get carried back again," Robert went on. "Are you really all right, Mother?"

Eliza struggled to sit up, "I'm fine, children, just fine. Let's praise the Lord for saving my life." And there on the sand the three bowed their heads while Mother thanked her heavenly Father for His protective care.

"Now, boys, help Mother to her feet, and we'll be on our way. My boots will have to dry out before I can wear them again."

Soberly the two boys walked beside Mother the rest of the day, not daring to let her out of their sight. They were worried about her, for she seemed so quiet, as though lost in a daze—sometimes talking to herself and other times saying softly, "Yes, Lord, that's how it was, Lord."

As for Eliza, the walk to Monrovia had turned into a battle—not between herself and the elements, but between her and her God.

In all her 26 years, she had never doubted her call, even when the mission had stopped supporting her, or when she had found the buildings destroyed and the children gone. Her tears had all been for those who had never heard of the love of Christ, hopeless in their fear of evil spirits, and for the tribal children without opportunity to learn. But she had never wept for herself.

She had often taught her children, "Before we can get to the good things of life, we got to enjoy some hard things."

But now, nearing the end of her physical strength, Satan attacked her spiritual stamina, and she found herself wondering whether she had made the right decisions. Maybe she should have returned to America with Susie years ago. Maybe God had not intended a woman to stay in Africa alone.

She had never taken a new step without earnest prayer, but no decision had been as difficult as when Mr. George had asked her to marry him. Every detail of her first meeting with him still stood out clearly in her mind. As she plodded along, her mind relived that morning more than 12 years earlier.

Mr. George had been staying with her friends, the Reeves', in Fortesville. Eliza had walked to Fortesville that morning in 1916 to take a boat to Buchanan to get some supplies. She was pleased to see Mr. Reeves and his wife making arrangements to hire a boat.

Mr. Reeves had called to her when he saw her approaching. "Are you going to Buchanan this morning too? Why don't you come in our boat? There are only three of us."

Eliza was grateful, for sharing the cost of the boat would leave more of her dwindling resources for the things she had to buy for the school. There had been no money from the Convention since the news of the split. Besides, she enjoyed being with the Reeves', who had treated her like a daughter ever since her arrival in Liberia.

As Eliza stepped into the boat she noticed a slight man, dressed in a dapper gray suit, sitting in front of Mrs. Reeves. His generous mustache seemed too large for his face, and the little patch of hair on top of his head looked like a rabbinical cap. But his smile was open and his eyes were warm and friendly as he greeted Eliza.

Mrs. Reeves turned to her: "Miss Davis, I'd like you to meet our house guest, Mr. G. Thompson George. He came to call on you and Miss Taylor yesterday, but you were gone on a preaching tour."

"How do you do, Mr. George?" Eliza responded as she settled on the plank in front of Mrs. Reeves. "Miss Taylor told me of your visit. I'm so sorry I wasn't at home to welcome you to our little mission."

Mr. George reached his hand across Mrs. Reeves to acknowledge Eliza's greeting. "I'm pleased to make your acquaintance, Miss Davis. I traveled with some friends of yours on the ship coming from Liverpool through the Suez Canal. Do you remember Rev. and Mrs. Konigmaaker? They said they had been on the same ship with you from the States to Liverpool."

An animated conversation followed as Eliza and Mr. George talked of their mutual friends. The rest of the journey downstream passed quickly as Mr. George recounted tales of his travels from British Guiana to Europe and Africa.

G. Thompson George had studied medicine as a young man in Guiana, but before completing his degree left school to take a job in a bank. At 44 years of age he learned of an opportunity to work for a Portuguese firm in East Africa.

"I always wanted to visit Africa," he explained in his high-pitched English accent, obviously enjoying the rapt attention of the two ladies and the congressman. "I took the opportunity to spend some time in Europe visiting London and Italy—places I had studied about in school."

Eliza was impressed with Mr. George's broad experience and education, so unlike blacks in her own country. In later years she would explain her reaction. "You see, the English freed their slaves before the Americans, so Mr. George had wonderful training. He had more sense than I had."

Before reaching Fortesville the travelers learned that Mr. George had sailed through the Suez and down the East Coast of Africa, where he had worked on a sugar plantation in Mozambique. There he became disillusioned with colonial oppression as he saw the sugar growers uproot whole villages, destroying their crops and homes to clear the land for sugar.

He said the end came when he went to oversee the burning and clearing of some lands for the company. A tearful tribal woman stood watching her halfgrown field of corn going up in flames. Hysterically she began shouting at him in her tribal tongue. One of his native assistants explained, "She asks why you are doing this to her when your skin and hair are the same as hers."

Before leaving Mozambique, Mr. George visited the grave of David Livingstone's wife. Standing at the tomb, his own heart was overwhelmed that this white woman had sacrificed her life for his brothers in Africa. Though George had become a Christian as a child, he vowed to serve the Lord as he stood at the graveside, and the desire to be a missionary in Africa filled his heart.

"So you see, Miss Davis, I've come to Liberia to find a place to serve God, just as you have. I'm working in Buchanan now, but only until I can make other arrangements."

It seemed all too soon to Eliza that the boat was pulling up to the shore in Buchanan, and the little party climbed out. Eliza said goodbye to the Reeves', but when she turned to thank Mr. George for the interesting journey, she added, "You really should put your adventures down in a book, Mr. George. In fact, you ought to visit the United States to lecture and inspire the Negro youth of America."

Eliza and her children hurried off to take care of her business in town, and the morning's encounter was soon out of her mind.

Two days later a messenger came from Fortesville with a letter for Eliza. An unwilling fear clutched her heart. Had the Reeves' received word from the Convention that she would have to leave BIA? Eliza took the letter into the hut, where she could open it alone.

But the letter was not from the Reeves' or even about the Convention.

It was from Mr. George, and Eliza read with growing dismay:

> Dear Miss Davis,
> As I told you, I have selected Liberia as my field for service. There has risen in my heart an undying love for you, and this comes soliciting in return

your affection in the consummation of the solemn vow at the sacred altar in the holy state of matrimony.

> Your servant,
> G. Thompson George

Eliza stared unseeing at the picture Mr. George had enclosed of himself. "What have I done?" she thought. "How could he have jumped to such a conclusion?" She tried to recall her every word and gesture on the journey to Buchanan to see if she had given him any encouragement, but could think of nothing.

"I only did what any friendly person would do," she consoled herself. "He wanted to tell us all about his adventures, and all I did was listen."

Then she remembered her parting suggestion that he write a book and visit America. Could he possibly have interpreted those simple words of encouragement as something more than that?

The messenger was waiting for an answer, and Eliza wanted to settle the matter there and then. She sat down at the kitchen table to draft a reply. The words would not come easily. How could she refuse him without hurting his feelings? But no, she had to make it clear in no uncertain terms that she was not interested in marriage, so he could not mistake her friendship for something else again.

In her bold, clear handwriting, Eliza began:

> Dear Mr. George:
> Thank you for your letter which was delivered to me this morning. I am returning it together with the picture you enclosed. I feel I must explain that had I the desire to marry, I would have done so before leaving America. I didn't come here to marry. I came here to work for the salvation of the souls of these natives, and nothing will deter me from my course.
> Your sister in Christ,
> Eliza L. Davis

"That settles that," thought Eliza as the barefooted messenger boy disappeared along the trail into the jungle.

But Eliza was mistaken!

With Susie's continual bouts of malaria and the growing response of the village people, Eliza's days were filled to overflowing, and she soon forgot about the incident with Mr. George.

As Eliza and Susie cared for sick babies, taught in the school, and preached in the villages, the outside world and its problems seemed very far away. News of the World War between England and Germany began filtering out to them, but its impact was not felt until steamers stopped calling at Bassa ports. Mr. Reeves sent word that a German submarine had been seen off the coast of Monrovia. The war diverted food and other necessities away from Liberia, and even on the mission the women were beginning to feel the pinch as they found basic commodities hard to get.

When Susie Taylor returned to the U.S.A. because of her recurring malaria, Eliza was left alone, fully responsible for the children. Her usual resistant spirit seemed to break. The day Susie left, Eliza prayed:

> Lord, I am all alone. Susie's gone; the Convention has deserted me; what am I to do, Lord? Who's going to take care of these children? How are you going to save these poor native souls if I have to leave this mission now?

And for one of the rare times in her life, Eliza threw herself on the bed and wept in despair.

But her depression didn't last long, for Eliza was a woman of prayer, and in the long night hours as she talked with her Father, He comforted her. The responsibility of the children in the school, the church on Sundays, and the farm were all hers now. Added to these cares was the increasing concern about lack of food. With the rainy season upon them in full force, they were dependent upon the various root foods which they had been able to harvest earlier in the year. But 50 children, mostly boys, could eat a lot, and Eliza watched with alarm as their little store of supplies diminished.

To add to that problem, the rainy season was particularly heavy, and Eliza and the children were marooned for weeks on end at the mission, for the creeks and rivers between BIA and Fortesville were too broad and swift to cross.

At the first letup, Eliza sent the children out into the fields around the mission to see if they could find any cassavas or potatoes that had been left unharvested, and which were not yet rotten.

Maude had been a great comfort to Eliza, especially since Susie left, and Eliza looked upon her as if she were her own daughter. Though only about five years old (Eliza was not sure when she was born), Maude helped with chores on the mission just like the other children did.

This morning she was out in the garden digging to find some potatoes when she saw Father Reeves, as the children called him, coming up the path. He was the first visitor to the mission in weeks, and Maude was delighted.

Lifting her up in his strong arms, Mr. Reeves smiled and asked, "And what are you doing out here in the mud, child?"

"I'm hungry, Father Reeves, and Mother Eliza sent us all out to look for potatoes. But I can't find any." And the round little face crinkled up to cry.

Years later Eliza would recount how God met their needs at that desperate time.

"A note was delivered to me from Mrs. Reeves. She said she had been thinking about us during the heavy rains and was sending some rice. The boys brought the rice the next day, along with a note from Rev. Reese which asked me to send a sufficient number of boys to the beach to bring a 100-pound bag of rice. The boys went as requested and returned with the rice and another note from Rev. Liberty of Edina that said, 'At your convenience send more boys for two bags of rice, 100 pounds each.' We prayerfully thanked God for the showers of blessings he had bestowed upon us while we were marooned in the mission by the heavy downpour of rain."

When the rain had subsided, Eliza set out for Buchanan, hoping there would be some gifts from the States so that she could replenish some of the necessities which they had used up.

Arriving back in Fortesville, she stopped at the Reeves' for a visit, glad to be with friends after the weeks of isolation on the mission. Mrs. Reeves effusively welcomed her at the door, and Eliza wondered why she was making such a fuss over her. "Eliza, come in, come in, we have a visitor whom I'm sure will be happy to see you."

Eliza followed her down the passage to the sitting room, and was taken aback to see Mr. George having tea with Mr. Reeves. Embarrassed, she hesitated before entering, but Mr. George jumped to his feet and welcomed her warmly.

"Miss Davis, I was hoping to see you on my visit here. I hear you've been having quite a time out at the mission these past months. I was so sorry to hear that Sister Taylor had to return to America."

Recovering her composure, Eliza decided that she too could act as if nothing had ever happened between them. Once again Mr. George held his audience spellbound as he told of his experiences in Buchanan in his new job.

"And, Miss Davis," he added, "I've followed your advice."

"Did I give you advice, Mr. George?" Eliza asked.

"Yes, don't you remember you told me I should write down my adventures and publish them? Well, that's just what I've been doing. But I'm afraid I've run into a little problem. I have written my material out in longhand, but before I can send it away to be published, it will have to be typed. Would you know of anyone in this town who is able to type?"

Eliza hesitated; did he know that she had taken typing at Central Texas College? Perhaps he had seen her rattly old typewriter when he visited the mission, for she often left it sitting out on the table where she had been working at night.

Before Eliza could answer, Mrs. Reeves joined in, "You type, don't you, Eliza? It would be so interesting to type a manuscript of a world traveler like Mr. George."

So Eliza returned to BIA carrying a large envelope of closely written notes, promising to let Mr. George know when she had completed the manuscript.

In spite of her personal reservations, Eliza plunged into the task with great enthusiasm, finding herself avidly reading ahead in the manuscript as Mr. George unraveled his journeys around Africa.

The opening pages revealed George's concern for the black people, which echoed Eliza's own concern for her brothers. She found herself typing:

> It must be remembered that the pollution of a stream comes from its source, and any undue indifference suffered by the Negro, even when education and civilized in all parts of the world today, is due to the glaring and undeniable fact of his brethren in Africa remaining in heathenism, indulging in habits and customs repugnant and repulsive to modern culture and civilization . . . .
>
> It may be accounted a blessing in disguise; but to be candid, the Negro first became his own enemy in that he sold his own brethren as slaves to the white men to be transported as cattle to strange countries . . . . Today he stands wailing at oppression; oppression hard and

> rough, or oppression mild; a subjugate to a superior race in his own heritage ....
>
> To live and breathe as a man, what is to be done by the Negro himself? There can be only one solution and answer: Let the civilized and more fortunate Negro wherever situated agitate ....

Eliza felt as though he had read her mind; these were the very issues that had contributed to her resigning the position as matron in Central Texas College and coming out here to this primitive land. But she was even more in tune as she typed:

> ... increasing efforts must be put forward to enable his less fortunate brethren in Africa to be provided with churches and schools .... to disseminate the knowledge of the true God and His Son, our dear Lord and Savior Jesus Christ; the blessings of civilization, such as teaching thrift, industry, and economics, which could be applied and kept up by intelligent Negroes, who should feel it a pressing duty and necessity to voluntarily go forward in this great work. Those who cannot go should sustain pecuniarily and otherwise those who will.

"Amen, brother, amen," thought Eliza. She wished that Mr. George could go over and tell this to the churches that had promised to support her work in Liberia and from whom she had not received any gift for over a year. Maybe she could send a copy of the book to them so they would realize how important their help was.

> What have we as intelligent Negroes done and what are we doing for the uplifting and enlightenment of the race from which we sprung? If we have done nothing, let us begin now to do something by going or helping, for it is written, "If any provide not for his own, he is worse than an infidel.

Blowing her candle out for the night, Eliza kept thinking about the words she had been typing. "Lord, you know this is the message that my people need to hear back in America. How could I get them to read these words?"

And then a thought struck her—she would ask Rev. Kelly to publish the book for the Convention, and then every minister across the country would read it for himself! With that exciting thought, she fell asleep.

So engrossed was she in her work at the mission and the progress of the manuscript that when the letter finally arrived from the Convention, it caught her by surprise.

She had the letter out of the envelope and opened to read before she realized this was it. The letter from Rev. Jordan was brief and to the point.

> Rev. and Mrs. Daniel Horton will replace you at the Bible Industrial Academy. I will be accompanying them to Africa to introduce them to their new work. We will be arriving in August 1917. Please make suitable arrangements for their housing and for turning the work over to them . . . .

Not a word about where she was to go or how she was to get there. It had happened, and Eliza was totally unprepared for the news.

In the weeks that followed she moved in a daze as she prepared the children for the turnover. Putting Maude to bed at night, she would hug her to herself, wondering what would happen to the little girl if she had to go back to America.

Determined to present BIA in its best light, Eliza worked from dawn till dark, urging the boys to clear the jungle back farther from the huts, weeding and hoeing the gardens. Every evening she would gather them together for prayers, but with an added fervor that they learn their memory verses word perfect and sing their hymns without a mistake.

In the evenings she would continue far into the night, typing the manuscript; in those few hours she was able to lose herself in another world and forget the imminent arrival of the Hortons.

Sometimes Mr. George's descriptions of primitive peoples in Portuguese East Africa helped her to understand some of the enigmas of the village people with whom she worked.

> Natives of Africa as a rule have many fathers, mothers, sisters and brothers; and to the stranger it would appear a puzzle, but explained in this way—grandfathers, grandmothers, uncles, and aunts are known only as fathers and mothers respectively; brothers, sisters, and cousins are known just the same as brothers and sisters, and only by close examination could the relation be solved.

Eliza nodded in agreement; that explained why Jude has a mother upstream and another down in Buchanan!

Another thing that troubled Eliza greatly about the tribal people was their nudity. She would not allow a child to go nude on the mission, even if it meant cutting up one of the dresses in her own limited wardrobe to make a shirt or skirt. And she frequently found dresses for the women to wear who came in from the villages for medical help or to sell produce.

She wasn't sure she understood Mr. George's matter-of-fact explanation of nudity when he wrote:

> If any native should die in a village, there is a great lamentation among the family, all going entirely nude and sprinkled with ashes over their bodies. Extreme and absolute nudity is a show of great distress and is observed in their habits and customs irrespective of sex or who is about.

But a few pages later Eliza found herslef applauding Mr. George's observations of the natives on the Portuguese island of San Thome:

> There are a few wealthy and respectable blacks in this island, the majority being British subjects from Sierra Leone, but the condition of blacks on the whole, as in all Portuguese colonies, is deplorable, for strong drink, that dread curse of nations, is sold to the natives equally as food and results in crowded jails.

Eliza had already seen enough drunkenness among the Liberians to realize that it was as great a problem in this country as back in the Southern U.S. She had seen native men tapping the trees to make palm wine and had delivered more than one "sermon" on the dangers of strong drink!

One morning during these days of frantic preparation for the Hortons, Eliza received a letter from Rev. Kelly. Trying to console her in the tragic events that had forced the split, he gave her one ray of hope by suggesting that she try to find another piece of land which would be used for a new mission, and that once things settled down, perhaps the Texas Convention could assume responsibility.

Eliza's heart was light that day, though she knew that the Liberian Baptists cooperated with the National Baptist Convention here in Bassa County, and it was unlikely that they would grant another Baptist group a mission site.

That night Eliza completed typing Mr. George's manuscript, more determined than ever to ask Rev. Kelly to undertake its publication. In rereading the manuscript there was one section that made her angry, and she considered asking Mr. George to eliminate it.

It was a letter from an Anglican minister who had held services on board the Prinz Regent, on which Mr. George was traveling up the coast of Africa. Rev. Wright had sent a letter to the Church Missionary Society in London and sent a copy of the letter to Mr. George, which read in part:

> After the service I had a talk with the colored gentlemen and ladies (two had their wives with them) and learned the most interesting fact: the grandparents of these men were formerly slaves, who through the preaching of the missionaries who lived amongst them in the years gone by became Christians. When the slaves were emancipated, these, of course, obtained their freedom, and these, our fellow-passengers, their grandchildren, are sincere members of the Christian church going as missionaries of civilization back to the continent from which their forefathers were wrestled as slaves.

To this point Eliza had no argument. Wasn't she herself one of these slave descendants who was now in Africa as a missionary returned to the land of her forefathers? But the letter went on:

> As we joined together in worship on other occasions, our hearts were cheered to see the results of missionary efforts in the years gone by, and we were encouraged to persevere with our work amongst these degraded Basukuma at Nassa, knowing that our labor is not in vain, and that even if our few converts seem to come short of the ideal we have for them, yet we must not forget the long generations of animal existence behind them and the terribly strong hereditary tendency to vice against which they have to contend. Only after two or three generations, as in the case of our black friends on the ship, can we expect them to come up to the standard of Christian people in Europe.

To this "animal tendency to vice" Eliza took exception. Who enslaved the Africans, beat and mistreated the slaves, and lynched free men? If there was an animal tendency in man, it wasn't limited to Africans!

Eliza sent a message to Mr. George that the manuscript was completed, and the following Sunday he arrived in time for the church service. Eliza couldn't help but feel happy to see him; as the time for the Hortons arrival drew closer, she became more and more discouraged, and it was good to be able to talk with someone who understood.

As they went over the manuscript Eliza explained her plan to ask Rev. Kelly to publish it, and Mr. George readily consented.

"In fact, Miss Davis, I understand you have written several poems which are very good. Would you consider including one of those in the book?"

Laughing it off at first, Eliza allowed herself to be persuaded to show him the little notebook of poems and words to hymns that she had written.

Looking through the notebook, Mr. George pointed out one of her favorites. "Here's the one we should use, Miss Davis." In fact, I'll try to write some music for this—I've done a little composing in the past."

And so while he sat in the wicker barrel chair by the window reading through the manuscript, Eliza typed up her creation.

SEEKING THE LOST

There's a great responsibility upon me;
    The Lord now bids me go.
I cannot stay but must hasten far away,
    Where the lost are dying so.

Chorus:

Seeking for the lost ones,
Praying for the lost ones,
Working for the lost daily here;
Looking unto Jesus
Amidst heathen darkness,
Seeking for the lost daily here.

There are millions lost, who are groping in the dark;
    O how dreadful is their state!
They are lost in sin; may we not now seek to win
    Those dear souls for Jesus' sake.

Do you feel relieved when the Savior is displeased?
    See these dear souls pass away.

Jesus' life paid the cost; then why should they be lost?
Christians, help save them today!
O how sad to know that the heathen too will go
Into judgment without grace,
Lost forever in sin, in a world that has no end—
What a dreadful doom to face!
All are not sent to preach, but the lost we all may reach;
God has servants on the way
Who are working night and day; help them either go or stay—
Spread the gospel news today.

This was to become one of the children's favorite hymns in the years ahead as Eliza shared her burden for the lost with the students in her care.

As Mr. George started to leave to go back to Fortesville, he turned back to Eliza. "Miss Davis, I know you have many problems on your mind right now, and this may be the wrong time to bring it up. But my desire to marry you still remains. Won't you at least promise me that you will give it further thought?"

Looking at this kindly little man, several inches shorter than she and several years older, Eliza didn't have the heart to reject him to his face. "I'll think about it, Mr. George," she promised; "I'll think about it."

chapter eight

Mr. and Mrs.

"You'll have to watch the boys, Ora. They will waste hours on a Saturday morning gathering palm nuts if you aren't strict about how much they have to bring back before lunch." Eliza had been spending days explaining the running of the mission to Daniel and Ora Horton, her replacements from America.

Tension reigned the first few days after the Hortons arrived with Dr. Jordan. But a grudging admission that Eliza and Susie had done a remarkable job in establishing BIA in such a short time lent Eliza some relief. The 50 children had been on their best behavior, and even the rains had held off for those few days.

But in spite of the good impression, Dr. Jordan had made it abundantly clear that the National Baptists, Inc., had no commitments to Eliza; the Texas Baptist Convention was responsible for her. He told her she could stay at BIA until the end of the year, but after that would have to find another ministry or go home. How she was to find the fare for her return trip was up to her.

Though these had been difficult days, Eliza could not help but like the cheerful and dedicated Hortons. They were graduates of Morehouse and Spellman Colleges in the States and brought with them a wealth of experience and a love for the Liberian people. If she had to leave, Eliza could not have chosen a better couple to succeed her.

She and Ora Horton became especially close, and Eliza found herself pouring out her heart to this warm and loving person. The Hortons were distressed and upset about Eliza's future, but their hands were tied.

Night after night Eliza spent hours in prayer asking God for guidance. Even if she were to go home, she had no funds, and

He would have to provide passage in a miraculous way. But above all, she pleaded to stay: this was her life's work, and she had only been in Africa four years.

One night as she knelt beside her bed agonizing in prayer, she seemed to hear a still, small voice beside her saying, "Daughter Eliza, do not be discouraged, for I have another field of fruitful service for you. Trust me, and I will guide you."

Praising God, she got up from her knees, confident that the God who had led her to Africa would keep her here.

In the weeks that followed, Eliza continued to work among the women and children in the villages. The work that she and Susie had begun among the Bassa Baptist women was bearing fruit. The women's convention was to meet in Buchanan in December, and at that time the women were to bring in their pledges for the work of BIA.

Though Eliza was confident that God had assured her she could stay in Africa, there seemed to be no answer to the problem of where and how. One day in the midst of this dilemma, Mr. George appeared at the mission, this time to announce that he was leaving for Sinoe County, some 100 miles further south on the Liberian coast, where he had been offered a job.

There was a small settlement of "civilized" people in Greenville and a few families several miles inland at Lexington, but outside of that it was untouched by civilization.

"Perhaps you would like to have me look for a place to start another mission. From what I have learned from people who have been to Sinoe, there are few schools for the tribal children in the area."

Eliza's eyes grew wide as she listened to Mr. George's suggestion. She had never thought of moving to a totally new area. "That may be just the way to obtain a site, and perhaps the Baptist convention would agree to back me there," she mused.

Then she realized that Mr. George was still talking, "Of course, you know, Miss Davis, that a single woman like you could never work in such a primitive area alone. Some missions have withdrawn their missionaries from tribal areas because it is too dangerous. You would really need a man to work with you."

She looked at him with growing astonishment, afraid to anticipate his meaning.

"If you would marry me, I would be willing to leave my job and go with you to help start a new mission."

Mr. and Mrs.

Eliza was astounded; how could he keep harping on marriage? Didn't he realize she was an old maid, almost 40, and really had little desire for marriage? And yet—could it possibly be that this was the way God was going to allow her to remain in Africa?

She felt confused and wished he would just go away and let her think.

Sensing her hesitation, C. Thompson pressed his point. "Miss Davis, I know you refused me once, but things have changed. Unless you find someone to help you, the Convention is going to force you to leave Africa. We could really work together well; you are a trained teacher with a wonderful way with the natives. I've had years of experience among them and know what it's like to exist in the rugged interior. Won't you let me go and try to find a place for a mission?"

Eliza needed time to think and pray, but Mr. George was scheduled to leave for Sinoe the next day, and he was pressing for an answer.

What should she do? She had given up any thought of marriage years ago. She couldn't imagine herself married to this little man who seemed so determined to have his way. But even more shattering was the thought of leaving Africa, where she so clearly felt that God had called her.

In desperation, as if to get ride of him, she blurted out, "All right, Mr. George, you take my letter to the authorities requesting permission to begin work in Sinoe. And, if they agree," she heard herself saying, "I'll marry you."

In the weeks that followed Eliza vacillated between utter disbelief that she could have committed herself to such a course of action, and complete assurance that nothing would come of Mr. George's wild plan. "But if he fails, what do I do?"

She would argue with God long into the night. "Help me, Father; You see what a confusion I'm in. Make it plain what You want me to do."

As the weeks went by, Eliza continued to immerse herself in the pressing responsibilities of the mission and was able to push her personal dilemma out of her mind most of the time. The Bassa Baptist Women's Convention would be held in December, and Eliza trained a group of BIA children to go to Buchanan to sing at the convention. How thrilled she was to see hundreds of Bassa and Americo-Liberian women meeting together, something which had never happened before.

Eliza spoke with unusual power and conviction to the women about her ministry at BIA. In the offering that followed her message, the women met their goal of $500 for BIA, and for the first time since its inception the school had a financial balance.

One day toward the end of the convention, as Eliza was in her room in the house where she was staying, someone called out to her, "Miss Davis, there's a gentleman asking to see you."

Her heart leaped to her throat; intuitively she knew it must be C. Thompson George, though she had heard nothing from him in the weeks since he had left for Sinoe.

Their meeting was strained, and Eliza tried to avoid meeting his eyes. Groping for words, Eliza found it difficult to make small talk. But as they walked together along the beach past the wooden police station and straggling row of houses up on stilts, Mr. George, expansive as ever, told her of his trip to Sinoe.

"It's far less civilized than here. There are no roads at all into the interior from the coast; to get anywhere you just have to cut your way through the jungle and across swamps. There are dozens of tribal villages within a few miles of Greenville, but few schools or churches.

"Steamers do stop in Greenville now and again. It's a small port town and trading center for tribal people bringing their produce to market. There are a number of Americo-Liberian families who have settled there.

"But the Krus are still defying the government, and there is a lot of fighting going on. In fact, I heard that the Kru warriors still occasionally resort to eating their captured enemies."

Unable to restrain herself, Eliza blurted out, "Were you able to get permission for me to start a mission there, Mr. George?"

"Yes, we were able to talk with the chiefs in the area, and they have agreed to set aside 75 acres for a mission school. And so," Mr. George went on, "I did what you told me to do, Miss Davis."

Feigning ignorance, Eliza asked apprehensively, "And what was that, Mr. George?"

"Why, you know you told me if I came back with permission to start a mission, you would marry me, and we would go together to work in Sinoe. I brought the letter and," tapping his breast pocket, "here is the marriage license."

Eliza stopped in her tracks. "Why, Mr. George—I, ah—I'm not sure. You know I've never been married before, and now you tell me to marry you just all of a sudden like this?"

For a moment C. Thompson George lost patience and threw up his hands, sharply responding, "Look here, Miss Davis, you made the plan, I didn't. I simply did what you asked me to do."

Then, seeing her distraught face, he realized how upset she was. "I'm sorry, I didn't mean to rush you. But you did suggest I could get a marriage license if I found a place for us to work, didn't you?"

For the first time Eliza looked straight into Mr. George's face and saw the pleading look in his eye. Suddenly it all fell into place. Though she didn't love this little man with his English accent and his vast experience, she did respect and admire him. He *was* a fine Christian, and so intelligent. And he was offering her the only hope to remain in Africa. Yes, they could work well together. Perhaps God wanted her to be married after all.

Reaching out to touch him for the first time, Eliza put her hand on his arm and heard herself saying, "Well, all right, Mr. George. I did make the plan, and you did your part. I believe God has shown me that I should marry you."

On the 12th of January, 1918, Eliza Loretta Davis and Charles Thompson George were united in marriage at the Baptist Church in Hartsford in Bassa County. Rev. James Clark officiated.

The bride wore a white duck dress she had brought with her from America, and the Hortons were her only attendants. The matronly looking bride seemed to be in a daze as she came out of the church, as if she weren't sure this was all happening to her.

Only when the children from the mission crowded around shouting loudly and cheering, calling "Congratulations, Mother Davis!" did the reality strike her.

Stooping to hug them as they crowded around her, she said, "Now, children, you have to remember, I'm not Mother Davis anymore. From now on you'll have to call me Mother George."

And she had been "Mother George" or "Mother Eliza

George"* for more than 12 years now—12 difficult years of struggle, but 12 good years too. "Lord," she admitted, "You kept Your promise and gave me my work to do here in Sinoe. No, Lord, it was no mistake. Here's where I belong, and I would never have made it without Mr. George. Just bless him wherever he is today, and help him not to worry about us back here in Liberia." And then she added for the hundredth time that day . . . "and help us to get to Monrovia on time."

---

*The name "Mother Eliza" will continue to be used in this book for the sake of reader identification.

chapter nine

Why Did You Wait So Long?

Memories continued to flood Eliza's mind as she pushed her weary body along. Her near-brush with death seemed to heighten her sense of detachment, and she plodded along for long periods lost in the past, unaware of her surroundings.

Her wedding had always seemed vague and unreal to her, but her "honeymoon" was indelibly painted in her mind. Within hours after the wedding, she and Mr. George and Maude had set off for Sinoe in the only transportation available to them—a 20-foot-long, hand-carved rowboat. The pounding surf and hidden shoals were extremely dangerous. Only later had the Georges learned of an even greater menace.

On the very day of their wedding, Liberia declared war against Germany. A German submarine surfaced off Monrovia and sank the nation's only armed vessel, the Lark.

The officers from the submarine had then proceeded to the capital, where they had requested that all British citizens be turned over to them. When President Howard refused, the submarine began shelling the tiny thatch-roofed capitol indiscriminantly, and two people were killed.

Unaware of the international turbulence taking place only 100 miles west of them, the Georges had traveled for two days along the rugged coast. Kru sailors, skillful seamen for hundreds of years, kept the bobbing boat under control, and Eliza had every confidence they would reach their destination.

It was strange to think of herself as a married woman, but fortunately the final preparations for the journey kept her occupied until they left the dock. Once out to sea, conversation was difficult because of the wind, and Eliza was grateful just to contemplate the broad back of the Kru rowers who were taking her to her "life's work." Mr. George would just have to fit in as best he could.

The Georges were moving into Kru territory, which was occupied by tribesmen who had been the middlemen in the slave trade. The men wore the Kru sign on their forehead, a two-inch scar slashed across their face, which many believe identified them as "unsuitable slaves." Whatever the reason, the Kru had resisted slavery for themselves, while capturing and selling people from neighboring tribal groups.

During the early part of the twentieth century a movement of God's Spirit brought many coastal Krus into the churches—Methodist, Baptist, and Roman Catholic—though it did not affect the interior villages.

Thus, when the Georges arrived, they were welcomed warmly by the three churches of Zion Grove Baptist Association of Sinoe and were invited to stay in the home of Rev. and Mrs. Amos Witherspoon in Lexington.

The settlement, a few miles inland from the port town of Greenville, could hardly be called even a village. Its one dirt trail doglegged through the forest to the river's edge, with about a dozen two-story thatch and zinc houses set back in the underbrush. Several had been deserted and were being taken over by vines and jungle growth and were almost hidden from view.

The "civilized" residents of Lexington either worked their farms or held political posts in Greenville or Monrovia, while Kru fishermen worked up and down the coast. Their great fishing nets were spread out to dry between the wooden stilts under the houses.

There was no store, post office, bank, clinic, manufacturer, telephone system, tarred road, office, or school in Lexington.

There *were* mosquitoes, politicians, churches, ants, swamps, and heat! Round-faced children hung shyly to their mother's brightly colored lappas as the newcomers walked by to the Witherspoons' house.

C. Thompson George had done his work well on his earlier visit, and all the people were eager for the Georges to come and settle in the area. Shortly after their arrival, the church leaders took the Georges up-country to meet with the chiefs and village elders to arrange for a piece of ground on which to start a mission.

Many suggested that the mission be established near Lexington and be more accessible, but Eliza was adamant that they move farther inland. She wanted to be closer to the unreached tribal villages, even though it meant walking through miles of swamps to reach the mission.

After some deliberations with the chiefs of the Sno-tribe, a subgroup of the Krus, a 75-acre plot was granted in the name of the General Baptist State Convention of Texas in a swampy, malaria-infested area between Maneytown and Parson Village.

Eliza and Mr. George kept busy during the months while they were waiting in Lexington for the land to be cleared and several houses to be built. They started a school in the Baptist church for the children of the town, and a number of tribespeople allowed their children to attend as well.

Though only six years old, Maude demonstrated spiritual discernment far beyond her years. Mother Eliza proudly wrote in her autobiography, "At the close of school one evening, Maude had the children sing with her while she prayed for them and told them about Jesus. Many of them were converted and walked home in the rain to tell their parents that they loved Jesus and wanted to join the church and be baptized."

As a result of this incident, the Georges held revival meetings in the church, and 75 people were converted.

Even before the mission was ready for occupancy, the Georges had decided they would name it after their friend, the Rev. James Kelly, and so it became Kelton Mission.

The two conical-shaped thatch huts were finally ready; primitive as they were, Eliza and Mr. George happily moved the schoolchildren out to Kelton. This time Eliza had to admit that it was much easier having a man to supervise the farm and discipline the children.

Years later, when those children (now grown) were asked about who was the strictest disciplinarian, the verdict was, "Mother Eliza never struck the children—she would spank with her mouth. But the old man, he beat us when we didn't work hard."

And hard work was essential. Funds from America came very spasmodically; the Convention itself sent very little. Some of Eliza's friends, like Rev. S.A. Pleasant, who had been a fellow classmate at Guadalupe College, sent gifts from time to time.

Thus it was important that a good rice crop was harvested and that cassavas, edoes, potatoes, and other vegetables be planted.

Mother Eliza began what became her practice through her many years in Africa. The children were called together for singing and prayers three times a day no matter what they were doing and where they were working. Her strong, clear voice would ring out across the little station as she sang one of the old hymns like "Jesus, Keep Me Near the Cross" in typical Southern style, and the children would join in singing as they gathered around her.

Rice-harvesting time came none too soon in that year of 1919; the food supplies were just about gone, and Mother Eliza found herself praying for a miracle. The children proudly brought the first basket of brown grain to her from the field. They were led by Jimmy, whom Father George had named Jimmy George because he was his special helper.

In spite of 30 children on the mission to teach, to feed, and to discipline, Mother was not satisfied to stay at Kelton. The villages upstream from Kelton were more primitive and isolated than she had found in Bassa. Not all of them could be reached by canoe, and she took several of the older boys and hiked through the swamps, sometimes walking through water up to her chin or balancing on footbridges made of barkless poles worn slippery from use.

Speaking through an interpreter, Mother stopped in each village, calling the people together to tell them "about a Man who died for you."

The villagers were perplexed and confused. "Why did He die for us? We don't even know Him."

Mother explained patiently that Jesus died so that they might go to heaven, but that they must believe in Him and stop fearing the "country devil."

Sometimes the villagers asked, "How long ago this man died for us?"

And she had to respond, "Oh, a long, long time ago."

Then they scratched their heads and complained, "How come you're just coming to tell us this now? Our mothers and brothers and fathers have died, and they didn't know about this. How come you tell us now?"

It was almost as though her vision back in Texas of Africans streaming past the judgment seat were coming true, and with a heavy heart she had to admit that these primitive, unreached people had a right to ask that question.

The urgency of telling the Africans in the villages about Jesus drove Mother Eliza out day after day, even when malaria began to wrack her body and huge tropical sores developed on her legs from walking through swamps for many hours. Though she took her quinine faithfully, it did not always take effect, and when she could ignore the debilitating fever no longer, she would take to her bed while Father George supervised the children.

Many of the village chiefs became her friends and were honored to welcome her into their huts whenever she visited their village. Old man Maney, chief of the nearest village, often came to visit Mother and Father George, sometimes bringing his whole contingent of wives. Mother reprimanded him, "Maney, you've got too many wives. You should give up some of them, and give your heart to Jesus."

But old Maney grinned his toothless grin, saying, "Mama, you see me, I'm old. My wives are my glory. But I'll tell you what I'm going to do. I'll give you all my children and let them trust in your God."

Shaking his head, he went on sadly, "If I'd give away my wives now, I'd be made ashamed."

It was many years before Maney agreed to give up his wives and accept the Lord.

As the year 1919 drew to a close, the world seemed to move in on Mother. She had been in Africa six years, and the effect of heat, fever, hunger, and hard work was beginning to make itself felt. As she wrote to friends back in Texas, they began to read between the lines that perhaps it was time for her to come home for a rest. Mrs. M.A. Fuller, who was the corresponding secretary of the Women's Auxiliary of the Convention, encouraged several of the pastors to raise funds for Mother and Maude to return to the United States.

Towards the end of the year Father George made a trip into Greenville to pick up the mail for the mission. He returned to find Mother Eliza once again down with a malaria attack.

"Eldie," he called as he came into the hut, "I have good news for you. Your friends in Texas have sent enough money for you and Maudie to go back home for awhile." There was a strange sound to his voice, and he walked unsteadily across the floor as he brought Mother the mail.

For a moment Mother wondered if he was also coming down with the fever, but when he bent over to kiss her the reason was clear.

Eliza had not found the physical intimacies of marriage easy, but she attributed this to the fact that she had been an "old maid" when she married. But to have her husband smell of liquor repulsed her.

Pushing him away, she sat up in bed. "C. Thompson George, you've been drinking. What in the world has happened to you—a minister of God and responsible for all these native children?" The anguish in those deep-set brown eyes, ringed with fatigue and fever, touched George more than her accusing words. He had meant to bluff his way through, as he had been able to do for years in the past, but he couldn't.

"I'm sorry, Eldie, it won't happen again. Sometimes I get so worried about you and where we're going to get money to feed all these children, and in a moment of weakness I accept a drink. I guess it comes from all those years tramping around Africa myself, living with godless men. But I promise you I won't do it anymore. Pray for me, Eldie, pray for me."

chapter ten

Coming Home

"I been prayin'; I been prayin,'" Mother mumbled. But when the boys asked her what she was talking about, she didn't seem to hear them.

It was obvious to Tussnah and Robert that Mother was ill, and though they had hoped to push on to Monrovia by nightfall, they now began looking for a village where they might stop and rest.

Robert offered Mother a drink from their precious water supply and saw how her hand shook as she lifted the cup to her mouth. "You go look for a place where she can lie dowwn, Tussnah," Robert instructed, "and I'll stay with Mother." Taking her hot, dry hand in his, he gently pulled her along under the hot, relentless sun. Fear clutched his heart, for he couldn't remember Mother being sick before.

By midafternoon Tussnah had found a village a few yards into the jungle from the beach, and they led Mother to the chief's house, where she was offered a mat and a meal.

But to Eliza's confused and feverish mind, she was coming home—Mama and Papa were waiting for her, their arms outstretched to greet her. How they had missed her these seven years since she first left home! How proud they were of their "missionary daughter"—the first black missionary lady to go from Texas!

They wanted to hear every detail of her experiences, and Eliza kept her family spellbound as she told them of her life in Africa. They whooped together with laughter as she dramatized things in the way they knew so well. They shook their heads in sympathy as she told of sick babies and hapless third and fourth wives quarreling in the villages.

Mama and Papa looked more wrinkled and bent, but the loving sparkle in their eyes was proof of how glad they were to have her home. Jenny Belle had been married and widowed while she was away; other members of the family had moved out to establish their own homes. But they were all together now, and it seemed as though little had changed in the clapboard house in Taylor, Texas.

The nation, emerging from the war years, was enjoying a technological boom; electric lights glistened in many homes, radiograms blared, and movie theaters attracted crowds.

When Eliza had left America in 1914, the automobile was still the toy of a few rich people. When she returned in 1920, Mr. Ford's clone was everywhere, and road builders were unable to keep pace with auto production.

Some things shocked Eliza's victorian spirit—suffragettes, the flappers, and bootlegging. And what saddened her deeply was to come back to the racial prejudices and tensions in her own land, and to realize that the Ku Klux Klan was more powerful now than when she left.

But to eight-year-old Maude, America was a wonder world of fantasy never even imagined back on the Pepper Coast. She bounced endlessly on the soft chairs; she squealed with delight when Eliza put her hand on the ice block in the icebox; she pressed her fat little face against the window panes, which kept the rain out without darkening the room.

The trip to the U.S. had taken 5½ months. The first few months had been spent in Monrovia while Mother Eliza legally adopted Maude and worked on the necessary paperwork to bring her to America.

They had met the Hortons, who had come to the capital for a rest, and they had caught up on all the news from BIA. The Hortons told her that the mission was moving them to Monrovia at the end of their term, and she promised to visit them there on her way back from America.

It was good to be home with her family, but Eliza was already homesick for Africa and anxious to know how her husband was getting along back at Kelton without her. They had agreed together that he would stay behind to build a more substantial house to replace the mud-and-thatch one, which was already showing signs of disintegration. Eliza had hoped to be able to send him money for the building soon after she got home.

But she was beginning to realize that it might take her several years to raise the needed funds to return. Though the country was prosperous after the war, Negroes earned very little. Many black Christians were very interested in the work in Liberia and gave what they could. But most found it difficult to understand the needs so far away in Africa when their own financial and social problems were so pressing. In fact, many envied the freedom and security of their African sisters and brothers and could not comprehend the fear and bondage of living under tribal religions.

When Eliza had been home almost two years, she received a letter from her husband telling her that his money had come to an end and that he could no longer work on the house. He requested that she send him enough funds so he could join her in the States, and they would then visit the churches together to raise money.

Dutifully Eliza took her savings for her and Maude's return and sent it to Mr. George.

Sea travel in the twenties was slow and unpredictable, and Eliza did not expect to see Mr. George for at least six months. There were few ships coming directly from Monrovia to the States, and it was difficult to make connections without long layovers.

However, a year went by before he arrived in Texas. Taking a Spanish steamer to Mexico, Mr. George was delayed by immigration authorities there for six months. When Eliza learned of his predicament, she wrote for help to Dr. Frank, the chairman of the National Foreign Mission Board, Unincorporated, the breakaway group to which the Texas Convention belonged. But Dr. Frank replied that there was nothing he could do.

Eliza was at her wit's end; she had sent Mr. George funds in Mexico so he could maintain himself there, but that was depleting her resources, and she was no closer to returning to Africa than when she had arrived. Finally Mama came up with a suggestion: "Daughter, I think you should ask the advice of the white Baptist minister in town, Dr. Jester. He's so friendly and nice. And you know, white folks seem to be able to take care of such things."

Willing to try anything to bring the impasse to an end, Eliza contacted Dr. Jester, who in turn wrote the immigration department in Washington and obtained permission for C. Thompson George to enter the U.S.A.

Eliza never spoke of her family's impressions of Mr. George, and very few of her friends ever recall meeting him. But the

Georges did spend most of 1923 traveling from church to church, presenting the work in Liberia. Rev. George, as he was called by now, shared in the meetings, but it was Mother Eliza's dramatic storytelling and implicit faith in God which won them many friends. And little Maude warmed her way into countless hearts as she told them how she loved Jesus.

One of the concerns on Eliza's heart had been for the children back in Kelton, and she probed her husband until she knew what had happened to each one. Most of them she had sent back to their parents when she knew she had to leave. A few years break in their education would make little difference, since most of them would never have gone to school at all without Mother Eliza, and they could just pick up their studies where they left off when she returned.

Father George told her that a few of the boys, including Jimmy George, who had no parents, had remained at Kelton, and he had arranged for a woman from the village to care for them.

And with that Eliza had to be satisfied for the time being.

The Georges spent many hours discussing their financial situation. It would be so much easier if the National Baptists would promise to support their work regularly rather than having to depend on sporadic gifts from them and interested friends.

Eliza and George made a trip to Louisville, Kentucky, to see Dr. Frank, hoping that some agreement could be reached. But though the work at Kelton now fell under the National Baptist jurisdiction, since it was the parent body of the Baptist Convention of Texas, there were no funds available.

"You'll just have to go out there and help yourselves," was Dr. Frank's pronouncement.

The time for Mr. George's visa had just about expired, and the crestfallen couple returned to Houston to their faithful friend, Dr. S. A. Pleasant, who was the moderator of the Mount Zion district at that time.

Listening to their discouraging report, Rev. Pleasant agreed to help them. He contacted the ministers of the other churches in the district and encouraged them to help the Georges. In the remaining weeks before Mr. George was to sail, the churches gave enough to provide not only his fare, but to purchase carpenter's tools, farming implements, and other necessities for the mission.

Since there were other churches in the district still to visit, Eiza agreed to remain behind to raise more funds. How she longed to sail with Mr. George, to get back to her beloved native children and the tribal villages without the gospel!

She waited eagerly for word from Mr. George about the children who had been left behind at Kelton and about her friends and converts in Lexington.

When his letter finally came, there was disappointingly little news except to say that all the children had left the mission. But he did urge her to hurry back. He needed window frames and other building materials that he could not get in Liberia. He wanted her to purchase them in Hamburg and would meet her there, and they would travel back to Liberia together.

The plan sounded a bit strange to Eliza, but there was no time to get a letter back and forth, so she made arrangements to sail. She continued to hold meetings wherever she could as she moved eastward across the country.

In Louisville her plans fell to pieces. She was taken ill and missed the steamer out of New York. There was no way to let Mr. George know, for he was already on his way by then.

To a lesser woman the disappointments and irritations that had compounded on this furlough would have been a sign to quit. She had now been in the United States six years trying to raise money for herself, her adopted daughter, and her husband. The mission in Africa was closed and the children were scattered. The mission board under whom she served showed only halfhearted interest and gave little support. She was 46 years old, sick, and married to a man she didn't understand, but she was determined to return to Africa.

When she didn't appear in Hamburg, C. Thompson George used the money she had sent for building materials and sailed to America to find his wife.

Gradually Eliza's physical condition seemed to improve, and she and Rev. George began taking meetings in Kansas. But her trials were not over yet—before the end of 1926 she had to have major surgery; a few months later her mother passed away; and then her husband's visa ran out, and he had to go to Cuba to try to reenter the U.S. on a new quota.

With traveling and medical expenses, most of their money had been used up, and as soon as Eliza was strong enough, the Georges began traveling again. There were many opportunities to speak in black churches in Kentucky, Kansas, Nebraska, and especially Texas. Though few pledged to send support regularly, the people responded warmly, and the Georges felt they had developed a strong base.

The couple held their last meeting at the St. John's Baptist Church in Houston, that godly group of people led by Dr. Pleasants, who had come to their rescue so many times before.

It had been more than eight years since Eliza and Maude, now a young lady of 16, had left Liberia. It had been eight years of struggle, disappointment, sorrow, and hardship. Many times Eliza must have wondered if she would ever be able to return to her beloved Africa, but she never succumbed to the temptation to give up. God had called her to serve Him in Liberia, and she held onto this conviction with fierce determination, until the day she boarded the ship sailing east to the Pepper Coast.

chapter eleven

Cerella

All through the night Tussnah and Robert could hear Mother tossing and talking, sometimes to her Mama and Papa, sometimes to Maude.

"You've been a good girl, Maude. You have been such a help taking care of the little children. Why, I could never have taken care of Cerella without you . . ." she would mumble before drifting off into a troubled sleep.

The boys had heard the story of Cerella many times. They had been there when Maude had returned from a village one Sunday morning with a thin, sick-looking baby girl. She had announced that the baby's mother wanted her to be brought up on the mission. The mother had had many children, but none of them had lived long enough to walk. The "country doctor" hadn't been able to help her; every one of them died.

Mother's heart had been overjoyed when Maude brought the sickly baby back to Kelton. Though she had a few girls whose parents were Americo-Liberians and thus saw the need of an education for their daughters, few tribal parents would give up their little girls.

The boys had often heard Mother complain that girls were just like property—their dowries were worth more than $40 in goods: goats, brass kettles, pots, etc. Every little girl in the village was spoken for long before she reached puberty. Mother often tried to redeem the girls by repaying the dowry for them but was usually not successful.

But now a mother had brought a baby girl to be raised at the mission. Mother Eliza named her Cerella, and under her watchful eye and loving care she grew into a chubby, cheerful little girl who was the center of attention for all the children on the mission. Cerella never lacked for loving arms or playful care, and everywhere the children went, whether at work or play, Cerella was taken along.

Then in December 1928 another little girl joined them on the mission. The children had been part of a choir that Mother had taken back to Lexington to put on a Christmas program in the Baptist church.

Cecelia had come to Lexington to visit her grandmother, and when she heard the mission children sing, she longed to go to the mission too. Her father had disappeared, leaving her mother to raise a large family, and there was no hope for Cecelia ever to go to school.

As she heard Mother Eliza tell about the school at Kelton, Cecelia thought to herself, "I would love to listen to her every day in school and help her work around the mission."

On the way home after the program, Cecelia asked her grandmother what a child had to do to go to live on the mission with Mother Eliza. He grandmother replied, "I guess you just have to ask her if she'll take you, child. Are you wanting to go and stay with her?"

"Oh, yes, Grandma—I would be so good and do everything to help her. Do you think she'd take me?"

And so it was that early in 1929 Cecelia joined the group of little girls who shared Mother Eliza's two-room hut. She became a little shadow of her idol and listened adoringly to all she had to say. The next time Mother Eliza took a group of children back to Lexington to be baptized by Rev. Birch, Cecelia was one of those who had given her heart to Jesus.

Mother had a unique way of including the children in every part of her life. If there were financial needs, she would tell them about the need and say, "Children, let's pray; God will meet our need."

If she went to preach in the villages, she would take along as many children as would fit in the boat. Skimming along in the canoe, which she bought to get up and down the Sinoe River, she would teach them Bible verses and hymns. To this day many of those children recall the joy of pulling on the oars while singing heartily at the top of their voices, with Mother sitting erectly in the stern, clapping her hands while her clear, strong voice rose above them all.

She never walked to Greenville for supplies without a troupe of four or five children accompanying her, talking to them as if they were little grown-ups, teaching them all along the way. The journeys took longer than expected, for if Mother came to a village she would turn in and call the people together for a Bible lesson and prayer.

Sometimes she would tell the children Bible stories, gesturing with her walking stick and dramatizing exciting events so that they would end up standing in a huddle in the middle of the path, wide-eyed and intense, waiting for the dramatic outcome.

If they met another traveler on the path, Mother would stop and talk, interested in his welfare and never going on without putting her hand on his shoulder with the words, "Son, let's pray."

When she worked in the garden she set the pace, hoeing longer and faster than even the strongest of the boys. She would never ask them to do a task twice; rather, her children embarrassingly tell of how she would pick up the bucket herself and say loudly as she walked toward the river, "Well, then, Mother will get the water." The children would scramble after to retrieve the bucket, for it was unthinkable to let Mother get water herself.

They remember her ingenuity as well. One of her girls, Genevieve, recalls how she cared for her clothes. "The mission girls washed her clothes, but she never worried us to press them. She would fold them up and put them on the chair. When she was writing letters at night, she would sit on the clothes and then put them on in the morning."

Eliza never totally gave in to the heat of Liberia, for she continued to wear the modest dress which she had been accustomed to back in America. The girls who washed her clothes would be astounded at the "singley"—the all-in-one romper which she wore under her slip.

In spite of the constant lack of funds, the restricted diet, and the primitive living conditions, there was a happy spirit on the mission, for Mother's infectious personality and abiding faith in God established the climate. With all there was to do and no one else to help her, Mother's teaching time was limited, and the children learned the barest rudiments academically. But in reality, Kelton Mission was one big classroom in Christian living, with regular tests to ensure progress.

One such test came on a sunny day in late 1929. Mother had sent Maude out to the farthest field with some of the older boys to work in the rice fields while she and the younger children prepared palm oil. Maude had taken Cerella on her back as usual, so that there would be no little one crawling about, pulling over basins, or getting dangerously near the fire.

Suddenly Mother could hear the rush of feet and excited calls coming from the field. She jumped to her feet to see the children running back to the mission. As they got closer she could see that the girls were crying and shouting something about Cerella. A surge of panic came over her as she noted that Maude did not have Cerella on her back.

"She's gone, Mother. The chief and some of the villagers came and took Cerella back; they said they've changed their minds, and they don't want her to stay on the mission." Maude fell hysterically to the ground, wailing loudly, and the others joined as if in a tribal death watch.

The commotion and wailing brought the rest of the children running to see what had happened, and in a few moments a crowd of bewildered and frightened youngsters surrounded Mother. They were "children" to her, but many of the older boys, like Robert and Tussnah, were almost young men, and Mother realized she would have to calm down these potential young warriors.

"Children, let's pray."

Hearing the words they had heard every day since they had come to the mission, a sudden hush came over the distraught group as Mother committed yet another crisis to her only Source of help.

"Now you go back to the garden and finish what you were doing, and Mother will fast and pray for Cerella." Mother's peaceful acceptance came only from her confidence in God, for she knew that Cerella's abduction must have been with the advice and backing of the chief of the village, and it would be difficult to persuade him to return her.

It was not only that Mother Eliza had grown to love Cerella as her own daughter, as she had seen her develop from a sickly infant near death to a robust, healthy child, but she knew there was no hope for her back in the village; she would be "sold" for the price of the dowry to a man many years older than herself. If she were fortunate he would treat her kindly, but, as was often the case, she could be just one more slave among his other hard-working wives. There would be no opportunity for her to go to school or to learn about Jesus as her Savior.

The boys remembered how Mother fasted and prayed for days; they were used to seeing her do this whenever a special need arose or problems developed on the mission. These days there was little enough to eat at best; the produce from the garden had been used up, and there had been no funds coming from overseas for many months to purchase food. Every source of credit in Greenville had been exhausted, and Mother owed money to every shopkeeper in town.

So the children ate potato greens cooked in palm oil, or they chewed the thin layer of meat around the palm nut kernel for a bit of nourishment. But Mother denied herself even that sustenance as she prayed for funds to "buy" Cerella back or simply for her return.

One morning a man from the village where Cerella was taken appeared on the mission, asking for Mother. He looked frightened as Mother came out of her hut to greet him, calling for an interpreter.

"Sit down, son," Mother urged as she pulled a rough bench in front of the hut into the shade, for even the early-morning sun was oppressive. "Have you brought news of Cerella?" she asked as curious children began hanging around within hearing distance.

The man began telling his story in the rapid nasal Kru that Mother could not fully follow, though as she saw the children's faces break into uncontrolled grins, she realized the news was good.

Robert, who was her interpreter, began explaining. "He says he comes from Cerella's parents' village." Mother nodded impatiently, implying she was aware of that.

"He says Cerella's parents saw how strong and healthy she was, and they knew she would bring a good dowry. None of their other children had lived this long, and they have not been able to receive payments of dowry to help them get the things they need. So they urged the chief to bring Cerella back to the village. He did not want to do that; he said the village had asked you to take Cerella and bring her up and that there would be trouble if he went back on his word."

Mother interjected, "He's right, you know; he shouldn't have broken his word."

Robert continued, "But at last Cerella's parents convinced the chief to give them permission, and they decided to watch for a time when Cerella was away from the mission and out of your sight. That's when they grabbed her and took her back to the village.

"But that very day the chief took sick. Nothing our country doctors did would help him, and he got worse and worse. When he died, the villagers called the witchdoctor to find out why the chief had died, and he says it's because he allowed Cerella to be stolen away from you, and that we must give her back. I've come to tell you that you can have her back."

Robert remembered how happy they had all been when Cerella came back to the mission, but now as he watched Mother toss and turn in her delirium, he wondered if Cerella would ever see her again.

chapter twelve

Strength And Sorrow

In the morning Robert was awakened by Mother shaking his shoulder vigorously and urging him, "Wake up, Robert; we only have a few hours to go to reach Monrovia. The chief says he'll take us across the last river in his boat, and we can easily walk the rest of the way."

Mother stood before him looking refreshed and strong, her fever and delirium gone. Robert couldn't believe his eyes. "No wonder the natives call her God-woman," he thought; "I've never seen such a strong woman in my life."

And he scrambled out of the hut after her to begin their sixth day's walk on the beach.

Yesterday's trauma was forgotten as the three weary travelers set out on this last day's walk. There were signs of civilization along the shore now, for villages were closer together, and here and there they met other people walking the beaches too.

It seemed that Mother had experienced a special healing touch which had revitalized her, not only physically but mentally, and she seemed more like her old self as she talked to the boys, who still hovered over her solicitously.

Mother thanked them for their help and concern, adding how much easier it was at the mission now that some of the children were old enough to take responsibilities.

"You know, for awhile Jimmy George was the only boy Mr. George and I could count on. He's turned out to be a pretty fair carpenter, too."

Then, stopping to put her hand on Robert's shoulder, she added, "But I always get worried to see you children grow up and start loving girls." Seeing the boys' startled expressions, she quickly assured them, "No, I don't mean you've been loving girls, but Jimmy wasn't much older than you are when he started disappearing from the Mission at night."

Moving along with her hand still on Robert's shoulder, she went on, "One night I caught him leaving, and I just stopped him and said, 'Jimmy, do you have a woman out there in one of the villages?'

"Well, Jimmy was embarrassed; he knew how I felt about keeping himself pure until he was married. It's not that Mother doesn't understand; I know what it's like in the villages—all the children running naked until they show signs of growing up; everyone sleeping in the same room, and mother and daddy have to make love secretly after the children are asleep.

"I've also told the chiefs that it isn't good to let all the older boys and girls in the village sleep in the same hut. They tell me that there is always someone there to supervise because they don't want the young folks getting into mischief either, but you know that doesn't work. The temptation is there to satisfy that strong natural desire. But God doesn't want you to make love with a girl until you marry her.

"Jimmy knew that, and he tried to explain what happened. It was our fault for leaving him alone here on the mission when we went to the United States. The woman that Father George left in charge didn't stay long, and pretty soon it was just a few young boys to find their own food and care for themselves. So when the other boys went away, Jimmy told me he just went out and looked for a woman.

"I tried to get that woman to marry Jimmy. I sent for her, and when she came to see me, I told her what the Bible says about marriage. I told her kindly, 'Daughter, he's my son; I raised him from small, small. I raised him to be a good Christian, not to live with a woman without marrying. Why won't you marry him?'

"But she just looked at me angrily and said, 'He's just a small, small boy—he's younger than I am. I can't marry him.'

"Now, boys, you remember what Mother tells you: God doesn't want you to live with a woman until you're married. You pray and ask God to help you resist temptation; and when you're old enough, Mother will help you find a nice young miss to marry."

The boys had heard Mother talk like this many times, but they were so relieved to see her back to her old self again that they listened attentively and assured her that they would do as she said.

As the day wore on, the weariness of the week engulfed them once again, and they seemed to keep going by sheer force of will. By the time they reached the first row of houses on the edge of the city, candles were flickering in the windows, and people were sitting outside around the doorways enjoying a small respite from the day's heat.

Though the Hortons were never forewarned of Mother's coming, whenever they saw her walking up the path to their rambling, two-story wooden house, the entire family would rush out to greet their beloved friend. But on this Sunday night they did not see her until she staggered up the steps to the veranda; she would have collapsed had not Ora Horton reached out to grab her.

Shocked by Mother's emaciated appearance, Ora hustled her up to bed, shouting instructions that the boys be given something to eat before giving them water to wash.

Ora tenderly bathed Mother's blistered and bleeding feet and treated them with one of her homemade remedies before wrapping them in soft bandages. "Eliza, what have you done to yourself?" she chided as she helped her into clean nightclothes and brushed her hair, which was stiff with sand and salt.

The two old friends talked for a few minutes, but Ora could see that Eliza was too exhausted to stay awake. Pulling the covers up over her, she said comfortingly, "Now you go to sleep. I'll see to the boys downstairs, and we can talk in the morning."

But Eliza half rose from the bed as she called after her departing friend, "Dearie, wake me up at daybreak—there's a steamer leaving for Sinoe tomorrow morning at ten, and I must get to the post office before then, or else this long trip will have been wasted."

The wooden post office with its rickety steps leading to the second floor sat along the only asphalt road in Monrovia. Since there were very few cars in Liberia in 1930, vendors used the street to display their wares—cassavas piled high in enamel basins, colorful lengths of cloth draped over poles, fat green plantains and mangoes. Pedestrians milled on the street, visiting shops near the waterfront—the big wooden stores of the English, German, and Dutch companies and the small huts of the Syrians. There were a few telephone poles tilting dangerously along the main street and out toward the one motor road leading to the Firestone Rubber Plantation, but there was no telephone service in the city.

Eliza and the boys stood on the wooden veranda of the post office, waiting for the doors to open. Ora had provided fresh stockings to keep her boots from rubbing, but Tusnah's bare, blistered feet were swollen and sore, and even the four-mile walk from the Hortons' home to the post office had been difficult. Fortunately, the landing area for the steamer, which they were planning to board by ten o'clock, was not far away.

When Eliza reached the counter, she thrust the notification of the postal orders into the hands of the clerk. "Daughter, we must get this money cashed right away so we can take the steamer back to Sinoe this morning. Be a sweet child, and take care of it as fast as you can for Mother."

Mother had a way of charming people so that they helped her in spite of themselves, and even the clerk behind the counter seemed to move with more alacrity than usual in response to Mother's pressing request.

She pulled a smudged and thumbworn folder from under the counter and began checking through the shuffle of papers, which seemed to be in no particular order. Meticulously she checked the number on Mother's notice with each dog-eared paper while Mother's anxiety mounted.

When she reached the bottom of the folder, the girl tried to reassure Mother, "It's probably stuck to something else—I'll go through them again."

After another fruitless search she called to a clerk who had just come to work, asking if she had seen the postal orders for Mrs. Eliza Davis George.

The young clerk languidly ambled over to the counter, tiny drops of perspiration glistening on her honey-colored skin.

"Don't you remember? That's the one that was lying around here for months, and nobody came to cash it. I sent it back to New York on the steamer last week."

The 200-mile journey back to Kelton was a blurred agony of hopelessness, pain, disappointment, and dogged weariness which made every step a monumental effort. Tussnah broke down at the post office, refusing to return by way of the beach. Mother finally allowed him to remain in Monrovia to seek out a relative who had a job in the city, but Robert would not desert her.

Years later Eliza described the hell of those days in deceptively simple terms: "We walked all day until about two o'clock the next morning. My feet were blistered so badly that we stopped at a civilized place on the coast and were permitted to rest on the porch.

"The next day we walked until about nine o'clock that night. My shoes were entirely worn out by this time, and by chance we came to a house out in the woods. I was unable to take another step." Mental and physical exhaustion had finally overtaken her indomitable spirit.

Eliza and Robert stayed at "the house" for the whole next day. What guardian angels ministered to them, who came to their rescue and organized a hammock for her to be carried to the sea, perhaps even Eliza herself did not know. It seems that by now utter exhaustion and exposure to the searing tropical heat gave those days a dreamlike quality, and its pain, like childbirth, was later mercifully forgotten.

Finally defeated, Mother arranged to borrow $9.60 from a Mr. Dingwall to hire a canoe to take them down the coast to the mission.

There is no record of how the children reacted to this devastating blow, but we do know that Mother's usual optimism and faith prevailed. In her autobiography she recorded the happy ending.

"We returned to Kelton. Maude was sick but cheerful. She told me how the Lord had blessed the boys to obtain deer meat given to them by some hunters.

"The Lord then blessed us by providing us with a good revival among the mission children. Most of them were happily converted. The boys cleared land and planted enough rice to keep hunger away."

Though many of her "children" tell of the walk to Monrovia and the devastating disappointment that awaited Mother Eliza when she got there, no one recalls that the money ever arrived. But the incident in no way daunted this courageous woman from her ministry among the Kru villages, and life in Kelton went on pretty much as it had before.

chapter thirteen

Born in A Cassava Patch

Just eight miles north of Kelton, in the tribal village of Seedor, another drama was playing itself out which would eventually have great effect upon Mother Eliza's ministry.

My parents tell me they had given me up for dead; my thin little body was covered with boils from head to foot, and I cried day and night in spite of everything my mother tried to do for me.

My mother, Nyonabe, blamed herself. Hadn't she foolishly gone to the fields to harvest cassava when her time was near instead of staying close to the washhouse, where any decent woman should deliver?

Nyonabe had sensibly delivered her first two sons in the thatch washhouse, squatting on the dirt floor with the rest of the village women standing around to give emotional support. No man had had to come near to help in the final thrusts of body, which forced a man-child onto the wet ground; no sound issued from her lips. And when the afterbirth finally came forth, the women cheered and ululated to announce the joyous news.

But when I was born, Nyonabe was in the cassava field. There was no time to cover her body with mud to keep her cool during the long delivery. Only Nyonnohtien, my father's second wife, was there to help as she labored in the hot, dusty field. When I was finally delivered, she named me Gbatoe, which means "cassava"—and from that disgraceful beginning, nothing went right.

My father, Marwieh, was even then a very old man—he had had many children before he was married; but in his later years, when his traveling days were over, he settled down with three wives. Nnyonube, the first and the youngest, was his favorite. She was the daughter of royalty; her grandfather had been Wale Wohjolo, and he was a "klosla" or royal peacemaker.

The story of the origin of the Klosla had been passed from generation to generation, dating back a thousand years or more. But every child in our tribe had heard of the two brothers, Saydee and Gidikan, who had fought each other and nearly annihilated the tribe, until one of the villagers suggested that they stop fighting and make the loser serve as slaves of the winners.

The villagers hailed this wise one as a peacemaker, and from that time forward his descendants were known as Klosla and were revered wherever they went. No one would dare lift a finger to fight another person if the Klosla sent his three-headed staff. It was as binding as the law of the Medes and the Persians.

My grandmother, Dehwlo, was Wales' favorite daughter, and even after she married my grandfather, the village would make special preparations whenever she came home to visit her father. Every household would bring out their wooden eating bowls and form stepping stones with them to the edge of the village so that her feet did not have to touch the ground.

In those days our tribe was wealthy. When they were first married, my father, Marwieh, had been able to care for my mother well. After all, he had been the first in the tribe to deal with white people, and the first to bring cloth to the village so that the women did not have to pound the bark of trees to make skirts. Marwieh had organized crews of tribesmen to go to the coast to work on ships which traveled to such far-off places as Angola and the Congo, and he brought back exotic things from the civilized world.

I can still remember my father telling me the stories that his father told him about tribal wars. "Gbatoe, those were the days," he would tell me with a sparkle in his eyes. "My father was a great warrior, and he was usually given the opportunity to bring home the body of an enemy. But he was very fair—when the body was cut up, he made sure that every warrior was given a piece, for to eat human flesh was the best way to stay strong." He told me grandfather wasn't really supposed to give him any, for he was still too young to fight, but he wanted him to be a warrior too, and so he would give him a bite or two of human flesh. He liked the palms of the hands best; they were more greasy than other parts."

But when the war between our tribe and the government forces started, those good days came to an end. The soldiers killed many of the villagers and destroyed our fields. The villagers fled, some to the coast and some to other areas, for our area was placed under martial law.

Life at the coast in Seedor was much more difficult, especially since my father, Marwieh, was now so old he could no longer work as hard as before. Many a day he just sat in front of the hut most of the time, watching his children play or talking with other men in the villages. And after I was born and became very sick, they spent their time discussing what had caused this strange illness in the Marwieh's baby son.

After hours of discussion, the man finally agreed to call the witch doctor to diagnose my trouble—a measure taken only as a last resort, for the witch doctor charged high fees for his services.

Of course I don't remember when he came to the village, but my mother often told me later how I screamed when I saw his face, painted with white and brown stripes, with red circles around his eyes. He was covered from his shoulders to his ankles with a grass skirt and had rows of beads hanging across his chest.

The solution was really very simple, he said. "Your nephew, Doh, who died last year, is angry with you, Marwieh, for not being there when he died. He has come back to trouble you in the form of this child. You must change his name from Gbatoe to Doh in order to appease his spirit." And then he gave my father a special ju-ju to hang above the door of our house to keep the spirit from entering.

My mother, Nyonabe, told me that after they began calling me Doh my boils began to go away. "It was worth the three chickens the witch doctor asked for his fee to have you healthy and happy again."

I don't really understand much about these superstitions, but I used to wonder if I wouldn't have gotten better even without the witch doctor's visit.

There was no one to tell us about a better way in those days. We were only nine miles from Kelton mission, but it might as well have been 90 miles, for we were isolated and cut off from the rest of the world at Seedor.

Then in 1932, when I was four years old, my father decided that we should go back home to Shaw, for the war in the interior had ended and news had come that the tribes in that area were living in peace once again. The whole village made the 40-mile walk through the jungle and swamp. It took them four days before they arrived at Shaw, only to find that the jungle had completely overgrown the site of my father's old village. I was to live there for ten years, until my father died. I was just a naked little native boy hidden away in the jungles of Liberia.

chapter fourteen

The Dream

Though Marwieh's village had moved north without ever having come in contact with Mother Eliza, word of the mission school at Kelton had spread to many tribal villages, and there was a constant stream of sick, hungry, troubled, and curious people passing through the mission.

One morning a particularly large group approached the clearing, and Eliza saw that a canopied hammock was slung on the shoulders of several men, who were walking with great care.

As she went out to meet them, she noted by their dress that they had come from beyond the Sno tribe area, probably walking for several days, and she greeted them warmly.

As the men put the hammock down, she saw an emaciated old man, his skin parched and dry from an evident fever. It was an effort for him even to open his eyes, but as he looked at Eliza he gave a start as if he recognized her.

The men spoke a different dialect, but one of the boys was able to understand and interpret for Eliza. One of the hammock-bearers stepped out to speak for the weakened old man.

"My father's name," pointing to the shrunken figure now lying on the ground, with the hammock serving as his mattress, "is Gidea Flukah. He has been sick for many months; the country doctors couldn't help him and left him to die. He knows he is old, but he has no peace. One night he had a dream—in his dream he saw a woman from across the sea. Somebody in the dream told him to find this God-woman, and she would tell him what to do. We have heard from other villages about this place, and that there was a God-woman here, so we have brought him to you."

Eliza did not suffer from false modesty. There was no question in her mind that the Holy Spirit had directed Gidea to her—she was the God-woman who had the message of life. And there was no greater joy than to tell him that Jesus loved him and had died for him.

When she had finished preaching, she got down on the ground beside the old man and took his burning hand in hers. "Old man," she began speaking, then turned and beckoned to the interpreter, "ask him if he wants to accept Christ as His Savior."

In a barely audible voice, Gidea expressed his faith in Christ, and an expression of joy transformed him as Mother prayed for him. When Mother explained that he should come back to be baptized when he was stronger, Gidea vehemently shook his head.

Puzzled, Mother Eliza waited as he and his son discussed together for several minutes. The son turned back to Eliza, unwillingly making the proposition: "He says he must be baptized now, before he goes back home."

Though Eliza made it a policy not to baptize her converts herself, and always made arrangements for a minister from Lexington to perform the ceremony, in this instance she sensed the urgency of the request. The party, now enlarged by the mission children who had gathered to listen, moved down to the creek, where Gidea Flukah was baptized in the shallow, murky waters.

He and his entourage left immediately afterwards to return home, and Mother never heard from or about him again.

But this experience deepened her desire to spread the work of the mission into other tribal areas, realizing that there were many villages only a few miles from Kelton which had never heard the gospel. After the long days in the gardens, walking to the villages, teaching, disciplining, and cooking for the children, she spent a good part of the night on her knees beside her bed praying for funds, for workers, and for the lost all around her. The girls who shared her two-room hut with her would tell of finding her in the morning asleep on her knees, or in a chair with a Bible on her lap, never having gone to bed the whole night through.

The financial burden was heavy, for her people back in Texas were hit hard by the depression and were unable to send gifts. Father George's letters were discouraging.

But her own optimism, faith, and determination did not permit her to think of defeat. Already several of the older boys showed signs of spiritual leadership and maturity and would soon be able to start a little mission on their own. Growing in the inner recesses of her mind was the dream of taking one or two children back to be educated in the United States; certainly Maude should have the opportunity for further training, since she had gone as far as a girl could go in Liberia.

Forces at work in the forests around her were to propel her into a decision sooner than she expected. Since the mission was fairly close to "civilization," the frequent tribal wars did not generally affect life at Kelton. Bur further in the interior the warlike Krus continued to flex their muscles in the last efforts of futility.

The Krus were the last of the tribal groups to succumb to the authority of the central government in Monrovia. Spurred initially by fear of losing their valuable slave trade, then later resisting the demands of hut tax and porter services, each side had been sniping at the other for more than a half-century.

But within the great Kru tribe were hundreds of subtribes who had learned to give and take as land areas became more populated and civilization's contacts caused disturbances in the delicately balanced "country ways." Land, women, power, taxes, or simply selfishness could trip the tightly wound hairspring to trigger a war.

So it was on a lazy Sunday afternoon while "the mission children were joyfully singing in their own tongue," wrote Mother, "a messenger rushed in and gave me a letter from Rev. Birch which read as follows: 'Come to Lexington at once; the natives are fighting among themselves, and they may reach you.'"

Eliza knew that women were pawns in tribal warfare; native warriors would capture women and girls, holding them for ransom or keeping them as wives and slaves in their own villages. With Mr. George away, they would be especially vulnerable to attack. The boys would most likely not be harmed as long as they were not involved in the actual fighting.

So she made a quick decision! Packing up a few belongings and leaving the older boys in charge of the mission, she took the girls and began walking back to Lexington. They would stay with the hospitable Birches for a few weeks, until the fighting settled down.

But while Mother helped in the Baptist church in Lexington, working among the children and the women's missionary group which she had organized when she first came to Sinoe, she received a letter from Father George pleading with her to come back to the United States. His time there had been fraught with disappointments—a serious illness had kept him bedridden some of the time, and he had little opportunity to present the work in churches. He felt that their only hope was to go back to the National Baptist Board to see if they could help them, and Eliza was the logical one to do that.

With continued rumblings of war, Eliza felt that this was probably as good a time as any to go back to the United States for a short time.

Her desire to take some children along to America now became a driving passion. Why not take two or three girls? Maude would definitely benefit from further education. Cerella was now a healthy and happy three-year-old, and Mother Eliza intended to adopt her as her own, since she had been officially given to her by the tribe. How wonderful if she could be educated in America! Cerella could be an example to Liberian women and would be able to train other Liberian girls in Christian things.

Mother wrote to Dr. Pleasants, who had always been a willing and faithful friend and was deeply interested in foreign missions. She explained the conditions in Liberia and her need to return to the United States, and asked if he could raise enough for her passage.

Mother also thought of taking Fanny, one of the girls who had been with her at Kelton for the past two years, but Fanny's mother would not allow her daughter to go.

But Eliza was unaware that God was working out another plan which would have long-range effects on the rest of her life. For Cecelia, now 12 years old and her adoring little shadow for the past two years, had heard that Mother was taking several girls to the United States, and she longed to be one of them. During the weeks of waiting in Lexington, Cecelia stayed with her own mother, who worked in town, but every morning she would be at the Birches, ready to run errands for Eliza or to offer her help wherever she could.

When Fanny's mother refused to let her go, Eliza, now obsessed with the idea of taking three girls to the U.S., asked Cecelia if she would like to go.

Without hesitation Cecelia responded, "Oh, I'd love to go with you, Mother. Will you ask my Mama?"

Cecelia's mother, who had long since relinquished any responsibility for her young daughter, voiced only one condition—"She musn't marry over there!" And it was settled.

Mother realized that she would have to apply for adoption papers for Cerella and Cecelia in Monrovia, and that this could take some time, so she decided to leave Lexington, trusting that her passage money would soon arrive.

Mother and the three girls left for Monrovia at the end of 1931 and stayed with the Hortons for almost a year while she worked on documents and prayed for funds.

When the money came from the faithful friends in Texas, it was just enough for passage for Maude and Mother. Undaunted, Eliza reasoned that since the Lord had led her this far, and since the girls were now legally adopted, God would provide some way. So she purchased passage for herself and the three girls as far as Cadiz, Spain, where she hoped to make connections with an American-bound steamer.

To 20-year-old Maude the sea voyage was nothing new, but Cecelia and Cerella found it a high adventure, eating the strange food in the dining room, turning faucets in the cabin, and sleeping on "shelves" up in the air. Mother Eliza never tired of telling the curious passengers that these little girls had just come out of the Liberian bush and were going to be trained in America.

Except for the failure of the engines for a few hours while out at sea, the trip was uneventful. But when they landed in Cadiz, they found that the steamer for the U.S. had left the day before, and there would not be another one for months. The stranded passengers converged on the American Consul, who could only advise that they travel overland to the Rock of Gibraltar in hopes of catching an Italian steamer due to sail for the U.S. on December 16.

Whether Eliza expected a miracle to stretch her funds, she does not say; she and the girls simply left for Gibralter, fully expecting to make connections. The ship was indeed in the harbor and not fully booked. But Eliza had not reckoned with reality, as the clerk in the ship's office explained.

"I'm sorry, Mrs. George; you need enough for three adult fares and one child; even if we stretched our rules and allowed the 12-year-old to travel half-fare, you would still not have enough money. You are short $200. There's just no way we can issue you your tickets."

chapter fifteen

Mother On The Rock

Gibraltar conjures up pictures of a romantic tourist haven at the mouth of the Mediterranean—an exotic, off-the-beaten-path photographer's paradise.

But as Mother and the three girls left the shipping agent's office that December morning in 1932, it looked exactly as it really was—a small Victorian settlement of seedy gentility, crowded onto the lower edges of the monumental rock out of which was carved the fortress which guarded the entrance to the Mediterranean.

Mother and the girls would have plenty of time to investigate the fortress with its imposing-looking guns facing out to sea from every aperture in the rock. But Eliza didn't know that then. With her usual faith and self-confidence she hustled the girls to the post office to send a telegram to her sister, Jenny Belle, who would be able to contact many of her friends and supporters about her financial need.

She was realistic enough to realize that mail was slow, and it might be four to six weeks before she had an answer, so she decided to ask for the full amount for passage—$331—and keep the balance of cash she had on hand for their expenses on the Rock.

Jenny still remembers that December morning as if it were yesterday. "I was just fixin' to drink a cup of coffee when Sister's cable asking for $331 arrived. I didn't have a penny to my name. I was so shook up I stopped drinking that coffee, and never drank another drop since."

In ensuing letters Eliza pleaded with Jenny to help "get her off the Rock," but to this day Jenny's voice quivers when she tells the story: "I had nothing to get her off the Rock with!"

While Jenny wrote daily letters contacting churches and pastors, and campaigns were organized to "get Mother Eliza and her girls off the Rock," Eliza had to find a place to stay. The Victoria Hotel, where she and the girls had booked the first night, was not for someone of her modest means.

Accommodations on the Rock were limited. Mother described the colony succinctly in her autobiography: "It has one cave, one prison house, one store, one theater building, one market, seven churches, two hotels, a reservoir, and a fort cut through the Rock . . . . There were only 900 inhabitants on the Rock of Gibraltar at the time I was stranded there."

Mother Eliza finally found a one-room apartment up several flights of dark, dirty stairs with faded Victorian wallpaper and an ancient sanitation system down the hall utilizing salt water. (Gibraltar has no fresh water of its own, depending on a reservoir blasted out of the eastern side of the Rock to collect enough water for domestic use.)

But God had provided a Spanish landlady who was kind and helpful and sympathetic with Mother's plight. Sometimes she sent up little tidbits from her own table.

But what Cecelia remembers best about the stay on Gibraltar were Mother's prayers.

"We were praying every hour. When the clock said 'ding' we were on our knees. When we got up it was half an hour; Mother prayed long prayers. At two o'clock we were back on our knees again."

But it would be six months before God chose to answer those prayers through the kindhearted friends in the Texas Convention. Mrs. Rose Chandler Jones, who many years later would work at the new Kelton mission in Liberia, remembers the appeal went out asking for funds to get Mother Eliza off the Rock of Gibraltar. I must have been very young, but I can remember that every large group or convention was appealing for Mother Eliza with her little girls."

Mother began receiving checks from various friends, but, as Cecelia comments, "We were thankful for the gifts, but the longer Mother stayed on the Rock the broker she got." And Mrs. Chandler adds, "We would send $25 or $30, which wasn't much, and they would have to live off that. They had to live while there, and they would use up the small amounts and not have enough to go."

But in spite of the hard times in those depression years, through the kindness of pastors like Dr. Newton Jenkins of Waco, Texas, Dr. J. Winn of Fort Worth, and others, Eliza finally saved enough money to make her bookings on the next steamer for New York. When she walked smiling out of the agent's office in April 1933, she had four steamship tickets and 25 cents in her pocket!

But Eliza's problems weren't over yet. In 1933 Ellis Island was still the major immigration station for the East Coast and also served as detention station for aliens and deportees. There wasn't much more that could have gone wrong as far as Eliza's documents and permits were concerned:

> —she had lost her citizenship through her marriage to Mr. George;
>
> —the two younger girls were seeking permanent residence without any visas to even enter the country;
>
> —she did not have the $500 bond required for the two girls who weren't citizens;
>
> —she had 25 cents to her name and no way to travel across the country to her destination.

A kind social worker on Ellis Island took pity on Mother and her three Liberian girls and advised her how to avoid deportation. The social worker wrote to Dr. J. Winn concerning the money needed for the party to cross the country to Texas by bus, and before long the money arrived.

At the the advice of the social worker, Mother wrote to Miss Perkins, whose father was Secretary of Labor, explaining their plight and why she had brought the Liberian girls to the United States for an education.

Then there was nothing to do but wait in the virtual prison environment of the Island. For five weeks Mother prayed, fasting much of that time. It was no surprise to her at all that the red tape and legal entanglements seemed to melt away, even to President Roosevelt giving a special dispensation releasing the girls without bond. Mother simply states, "While enclosed within the walls at Ellis Island we prayed with fastings, the Lord touched hearts of the powers that be, and the door was opened, and we entered the United States without bond."

The Greyhound bus trip across the country gave the girls a panoramic view of their new homeland, and in their excitement they didn't seem to notice that the farther south they went, the more they rode in the back of the bus and ate their lunches on their laps rather than at tables in restaurants.

But the welcome in Taylor was warm and wonderful, and they were soon engulfed in the loving clamor and noise of a large family of aunts, uncles, and cousins. Aunt Jenny Belle took the three girls into her heart; there were no children from her brief marriage, and Cecelia and Cerella filled an empty spot.

A thinner and older looking Father George was also there to greet them, and Mother realized with a pang that these past three years had taken a heavy toll on him, with little to show for his efforts.

As Mother expected, the girls made a hit wherever they went; people loved their droll accents and were impressed with their burden for the work in Africa. Mother soon had more offers to care for them than she could accept, but it was decided that Maude would go to Eliza's alma mater, Guadalupe College, while Cerella and Cecelia would stay with Aunt Jenny Belle. Rev. S.A. Pleasant assumed the responsibility of raising funds for their education, a task he faithfully fulfilled for ten years.

But the Georges realized that they needed a promise of regular support for the work in Liberia. They had labored in Kelton on and off for the past 15 years with no permanent buildings and no hired staff. Each time they left, the work simply closed down until they were able to return and start it up again.

Yet Eliza's heart was more burdened than ever for the native villages in the interior that were still completely untouched by the gospel. How she longed to consistently train the promising children in her care until she could send them out as missionaries themselves! She realized she could never do the job alone. But without adequate funds she had simply been eking out a hand-to-mouth existence, and though she never lost her faith and joy in the Lord, she believed there must be a better way.

As Mr. George related some of his disappointments over the past few years, Eliza realized that her people were suffering the extremes of these depression years; they too had been in the worst of positions, not only economically, but with growing social and political frustrations as well: many were out of jobs. Black churches in America were struggling.

Ever since her call to Africa, more than 20 years earlier, she had been convinced that the black churches in America should be responsible for taking the gospel to their black brothers and sisters in Africa. She had often considered risking affront by approaching the more-affluent white churches, but to Eliza, Liberia's salvation was a "family affair," and she believed that God would eventually help her American brothers and sisters to shoulder their responsibility in Africa.

But now time was running out on her; she was 54 years old, and Father George was in his mid-sixties. She had preached zealously and with deep compassion to every black church that would give her a hearing, and though many sacrificial gifts of love had been sent, no regular support had ever been promised since the split in the Convention in 1914.

Thus the Georges decided to contact white pastors in the surrounding area, explaining their ministry in Liberia. The Rev. R.W. Shirley of the First Baptist Church of McAllen, Texas, invited them to come for a meeting on Sunday evening in May, 1935. Eliza joyfully recorded the result of the meeting in her autobiography.

"The summary of our messages was that God had called us to work for the salvation of our people in Africa. We also told them about the girls brought from Africa to be trained in the United States, who would return to teach their own people after they were educated. Rev. Shirley was deeply impressed.... It was voted immediately to pay us $30 monthly support and to give us $250 for our return passage to Africa."

As though to vindicate the conviction that her own people would do more, the Lord also moved on the hearts of members of the Foreign Mission Board of the National Baptist Convention. The Georges attended the annual convention in Washington, D.C., in the fall of 1935 and were able to sign a contract with the Foreign Mission Board to work as regular missionaries at $30 a month. A further gift of $600 was promised for supplies and equipment.

It was difficult to say goodbye to the girls in Texas, but Mother assured them that as soon as they finished school, they would all be together again. The Georges left for Liberia with the hope that this time there would be enough funds to establish a more-permanent work. Even the thought of having to rebuild the thatch huts at Kelton, which surely had succumbed to the elements by now, did not daunt Eliza's indomitable optimism.

chapter sixteen

Go and Sin No More

And so it was back to Lexington to bide their time while materials were purchased, lumber was cut, and workers were hired. As always, Eliza threw herself into the work of the little Baptist church in the town, never satisfied to sit idly by.

It was in one of her Bible classes in Lexington in early 1936 that young Henry Williamson was converted. Mother gave Henry a part in a church program, and to his embarrassment he stumbled and stuttered so that his friends laughed and tittered at his discomfort. "But Mother was always encouraging," he says as he recounts the incident. "She just patted my head and told me, 'You did just fine, son.'" Henry Cicero Williamson went on to become the Deputy Speaker of the Liberian House of Representatives in his later years.

Within weeks after the Georges' arrival in Liberia, the first gift from the First Baptist Church of McAllen arrived, covering two months' salary. The gifts arrived regularly after that until the disruption of World War II. The women of the church sent parcels of clothing, medicine, and a sewing machine for the mission.

Even while the rebuilding was going on at Kelton, God began sending more mature, promising young people to the school Otto Klibo, a strong young fellow, volunteered to work at the mission and became a dependable stalwart over the years. Father George told him that if he worked well, he would make him overseer of the boys—but Otto went further and helped start a new mission in the interior in later years.

Though the promised funds from the National Baptists did not arrive immediately, a special gift of $300 from Dr. Pleasant and the Lincoln Association was enough to enable the Georges and the children with them to move out to Kelton. For the first weeks they slept on the damp ground, until plank floors could be laid in their mud cottages.

Encouraged by the regular gifts from America, the Georges had larger buildings constructed so that they could accept more children.

One by one they drifted onto the mission. Shelby Graham,

who became a respected Christian leader in the church, was brought by his father, who wanted him to learn English. He remembers Mother patting his head and asking, "Son, can you learn?" Shelby stayed with Mother for ten years, until she sent him to high school to learn carpentry. He became Mother's "manager of oil-making," responsible to produce several gallons of palm oil for the kitchens each day.

Lu Mason hadn't intended to join Mother at Kelton. She had been with her some years earlier, but after Mother returned to the U.S. she moved back to Lexington. She confesses, "I had a fall—I had a child."

She was struggling on her own as a servant in the home of a town family when her brother, who was already on the mission, urged her to come back with him. Lu refused: "I was there once, but I went back on Mother. I can't go to her now."

But her brother prevailed, and so, carrying a freshly baked loaf of bread as a peace offering, Lu gingerly presented herself at Mother's door.

Mother Eliza was happy to see her, throwing her arms around the fearful girl. Then, holding her away from her, she chided, "Oh, Lu, you did me bad."

Lu began to cry, sobbing, "I'll never do bad again if you take me back."

Eliza had a special ability to forgive and encourage new beginnings ("go and sin no more"). She understood their "country ways" background which made it so difficult for young people to make a clean break with the past. Perhaps she erred in being too forgiving and making it too easy for sinners to repent, but she would argue the point with you, for many found the way out of defeat to productive lives.

So Lu became Mother's chief assistant, handling money for small purchases, responsible for the storeroom, and supervising the washing. All of this freed Mother to do more teaching and preaching.

While Mother rejoiced in the expansion of the work, she watched with despair the deterioration of her husband. His poor health was aggravated by his drinking problem, which had had become so severe that it could no longer be hidden from the children.

Sometimes he would begin drinking early in the morning, and by the time Mother led the children in their morning hymn his befuddled singing would join in from the bedroom, dragging out the melody in an off-pitch voice for all to hear.

One of her boys remembers her running down the trail shouting after him for absconding to Greenville with mission money, but most of Mother's children only remember her anguished prayers for his healing and safety.

When he was not sick or drinking he still acted as a strict disciplinarian, lining the boys up in the morning to give them their daily tasks in the garden or on a building project. And in the evening he led the singing or taught music or history to the older pupils. With so much to do on the mission, classes in those early years were held in the evenings around the dining tables.

Without the promised funds from the Baptist Convention, the money was soon used up on the buildings, and Christmas of 1936 found Mother Eliza once more without funds. She had had to send Father George on an emergency trip to Monrovia for medical care, and debts had piled up again.

But in her childlike enthusiasm, Mother wanted to make Christmas special for her children, most of whom had never celebrated Christmas before. She described the preparations in detail. "The boys cut large vines from the surrounding forests and made four swings and a merry-go-round out of cottonwood, as well as five benches. The Christmas tree was decorated with beautiful white paper in which the medicine sent by Dr. Wharton was packed . . . . Each child received one card on the Christmas tree and two lumps of sugar. After the program that day five children were converted and baptized."

Early in 1937 a tribal family brought a seven-month-old girl to Eliza. The baby's mother had died, and rather than leave her in the jungle to perish, the relatives brought her to the mission. Though Mother had resolved not to take any more children until their financial picture improved, she could not resist this little one, whom she named Leetha in honor of Rev. Shirley's wife.

It seemed as though God was bringing her ministry to fruition in so many ways. Rev. James Bolo and his wife had come to her some months before, pleading that she send them to the nearby village of Plahn to start a church there. Bolo had been a Methodist minister for a number of years, but the denomination wanted to send him far from home, and he was not willing to go.

Impressed by the devotion and experience of the man, Mother longed to be able to help him become established in Plahn, some 20 miles in the interior. She told Rev. Bolo, however, that he would have to be baptized by immersion and become a Baptist if he wanted to work with her, a request he readily complied with.

In June of 1937 the first gift of $400 arrived from the Foreign Mission Board, and Mother was able to purchase supplies and send out the Bolos as her first missionary couple. With some of the money she bought cotton blankets for each child.

But her greatest joy continued to be the children and young people whom God was sending to the mission. One morning Mr. Joe Thomas came from Lexington with two boys who looked to be in their late teens. (Liberian children seldom knew their age, since calendars were not part of the "country way.") Mr. Thomas introduced one boy as his nephew and the other as a "country boy" who had been sent to work in Lexington and placed in his care.

Mr. Thomas informed Mother privately, "I want you to put more emphasis on my nephew because when I die my belongings will be for him."

Mother simply nodded in agreement, but she watched the two boys closely in the weeks ahead. The nephew was put to work in the kitchen, while the other boy, who had been given the "civilized" name of Charles Carpenter, was assigned to make fences.

One day Mother called Charlie into her room to commend him for his hard work. Then she added, "Son, we are here for the natives; the town people are already civilized. But I want you to be a good boy. Mr. Joe Thomas said I should have special interest in this boy, but I'm telling you I'm not here for the civilized people, because they are already educated. But if you work hard, one day you will walk into your own house."

Charles later commented that from that time forward he made a special effort to please Mother Eliza "And," he added wryly, "that other young man cannot write his name today."

Because Mother was especially burdened for the tribal children, whose parents were destitute, she never charged for tuition or food. Everything was provided for the children through her own provision from God. Over and over they would marvel, "Everything Mother had was ours; everything we had was from Mother."

When another gift of $200 came from the Convention later that year, Eliza purchased books and writing tablets for use in the schoolroom, and a bolt of cloth to make clothes for the children.

In describing how he became Mother's mission tailor, Charles also reveals the secret of her ability to stimulate her children to be more than they ever dreamed they could be.

Charles had returned from Greenville one day, where he had dealt with a tailor about making a pair of trousers. But as a "country boy" he was insulted, and so he came to Mother licking his wounds.

"I paid him the money, and he just abused me."

"Son, don't you worry—you will learn how to sew. When do you plan to go to town again? Mother will pay for it."

"I can start tomorrow," Charles replied eagerly.

The next day he went to town and wandered the streets until he found a tailor he could watch at work. Watching and noting every move, he hung around the streets for several weeks. When he went back to the mission, Mother asked him, "Son, where have you gotten?"

When he told her how he had been watching every move the tailor made, Mother gave him a piece of cloth and scissors and sent him back.

This time when they cut, he cut; and when he got back to the mission he stitched up the trousers. What a bungle—tucks and gathers in the oddest places—too short, too wide! Charles was in despair.

When Mother came to see what he had done, he tried to hide them from her, but she pulled them out of his hands. "Son, let me see what you did." And holding them up to scrutinize them, she added, "Oh, son, you are doing well. I know you will be sewing for the mission soon."

The next time Charles went to town he "looked good," and the second pair was much better. In a few weeks' time Mother was confident enough in his sewing that she turned the new bolt of cloth over to him, and Charles became the mission tailor.

With so many children to care for and her seemingly naive generosity, Mother seemed to live from "steamer to steamer," paying her bills and purchasing necessities when the money arrived—with long, lean periods in between.

One of the most encouraging developments on the mission that year was that they could hire a trained teacher to run the school for the children. A Sunday school class in Texas began sending $8 a month for a teacher's salary, and a Mr. Nepe, educated in the U.S., was hired. For the first time at Kelton there were regular school hours, with textbooks for the children.

Some of Mr. Nepe's former students followed him to Kelton. One morning Mother heard Mr. Nepe calling her to come out, saying, "Newspaper here." Wondering how a newspaper could have been delivered when there had been no steamer for more than a month, Mother hurried outside to see a young albino man standing beside Mr. Nepe.

"Mother Eliza, this is Newspaper, one of my former students, who would like to continue studying with me here at Kelton."

If the appearance of this pink-skinned, fair-haired African disturbed Mother, she made no sign of it. She had often-wondered at the cruel combination of genes which left the albino defenseless in the merciless African sun; but the few she had met in her years in Africa had been especially bright mentally, and Newspaper's first few words in his maturing bass voice fortified that impression.

Later, when she would try to get him to change his name to something more conservative, he would tell her, "I am the only newspaper in the world who has life, blood, and brains." He kept the Newspaper name and added George to it as he became an integral part of Mother's life.

In spite of all the changes of schedule and additional work because of her growing family, Mother never deviated from her prayer times three times a day, plus the Bible reading in the evenings before the children went to bed. Not knowing the language well enough to write songs in the dialect, Mother taught the children the old hymns she had grown up on. Before the breaking of the dawn, the children would wake to hear her strong voice singing HOLY, HOLY, HOLY. Before the girls rang the noon bell, Mother's voice would ring out JESUS, LOVER OF MY SOUL. One of her children recalled, "Wherever one was, no matter where we were, we came."

And it was in those times of prayer and Bible reading, kneeling around Mother as she praised and interceded, sharing with them the burdens of her heart for the heathen around them, that most of the children remember committing their lives to Christ.

And not only the children. Charles recalls that during that first year that he was at Kelton his heathen parents came to visit him and were converted. Later Charles himself baptized them.

Except for Mr. George's recurring physical problems, the years since their return had been the most productive and encouraging of all of Eliza's experience in Africa. More than 50 children boarded at Kelton; young leaders were emerging who were being trained for future ministries; though still of thatch and mud, the buildings were larger and more adequate for their needs; regular support was at last coming in; and a mission church was being planted in the interior.

But before the year was out, the first of a series of disappointments disturbed the work at Kelton: Mr. Nepe resigned over a disagreement with the Georges, and the school was left without a teacher.

chapter seventeen

The Living Newspaper

The little caucus sat around Mother's table, the yellow glow from the kerosene lamp throwing a soft circle of light which just touched their faces and elbows leaning on the table.

Mother had called in the three oldest boys after Mr. Nepe's resignation, knowing they would be most affected by the loss.

"Sons, I have a plan—when I was at Guadalupe College, many years ago, the principal asked me to teach some of the younger children because they didn't have enough money to hire a full staff. I think we can do the same thing here. I will teach you boys in the evenings after the younger children are in bed, and you can each teach a class in the mornings."

The quality of teaching was very simple, but at least the children continued to learn the basics of reading and arithmetic. Newspaper meanwhile used every means to quench his insatiable thirst for knowledge.

When the Liberian historian and eminent politician, Richard Henries (then county supervisor of schools for Grand Bassa, Sinoe, and Maryland counties), instituted a teachers' school for three months, Newspaper was able to attend. The second year all three older boys were allowed to go and were able to earn their teachers' certificates.

Mother's proud acclamation to that was, "Now I have qualified teachers—no more need of running around to look for them."

In later years Newspaper was to teach himself Greek, Latin, algebra, and geometry, as well as to become an avid historian. One wonders how he did it with his typical albino myopia, but his photographic memory needed constant new input, which his physical handicap could not restrain. Many of his students who went on to high school stood at the top of their class, even against the competition of students trained by teachers with far higher qualifications.

The school seemed to be working well under the older boys' tutelage, but toward the close of 1938 a whole series of events began to take place which caused the usually optimistic Eliza to write, "It seemed that we were being hedged in on all sides by trouble."

A shortage of water forced the children to draw their drinking water from the swamp. Though Liberia has heavy rainfall, it has large areas where the underground water table is inaccessible for drilling wells, and most people depended on streams and rivers or storage tanks. During the December-January dry season some streams dried up, causing severe problems, especially where there was a concentration of people, as at Kelton.

Mother believed that the children were exposed to "yaws" because native children who had the disease bathed in the swamp. But however it was contracted (medical science says this virus is transmitted by direct contact with skin lesions), an epidemic of the dreaded disease broke out at the mission. Children were covered in running sores all over their bodies, even in their noses and under their arms. They felt sick, with fever and chills.

Mother washed the sores with carbolic soap, not knowing that unless she used sterile methods she could infect other parts of the body with the virus. Under those conditions, Yaws was a long, drawn-out disease, sometimes taking two years to cure, but fortunately one attack gave lifelong immunity. There is no indication in her writing or from her children, however, that Mother herself contracted the disease.

As if her problems at the mission weren't enough, Cecelia wrote that she was planning on getting married later in the year. "You won't believe it, but his name is Owen Davis, just like your maiden name. People will think I'm marrying my cousin. But he's a fine Christian, Mother, and wants to be a missionary. Maybe someday we'll come to Liberia together."

Mother never shared what a blow that news was to her—hadn't she promised Cecelia's mother that she wouldn't marry in the U.S.?

Even during those difficult times Mother could not resist taking in a new child when he was brought to the mission. Joseph Doe, who today pastors a church in Monrovia, tells how his sister brought him to the mission early in 1939. At first Mother kindly but firmly refused, for there had been no steamer for several months, and she didn't have blankets and clothes for the children she had. But seeing Joseph's fallen face, she quickly added, "Come back in a few weeks; the Lord will provide."

When Joseph started on the mission, his first job was to go to the fields where the boys were planting cassavas and keep the flies off Father George as he sat in a chair supervising the work. Joseph quickly reassures, "Oh, he was kind, but not as kind as Mother Eliza. He didn't work, though; he just oversaw the work."

By this time neither laziness nor pride kept Father George from working; his health was fading fast, and he had little strength to carry his share of the work.

One morning in January of 1939 the children could hear Father and Mother arguing. He was determined to walk to Greenville for some "supplies," but Mother tried to stop him. She could see that he was in no state for the long, hot walk, but he stubbornly refused to take her advice. "I'll be all right, Eldie; I haven't been off the mission for weeks. The change will do me good."

All through that day as Eliza went about her business she fought a nagging fear which was so unlike her. She continued with her daily routine—teaching, working in the garden, washing clothes—but with a sense of detachment and using any excuse to be in the line of sight to where the path broke out of the forest. When darkness fell and she could stand the suspense no longer, she sent two of the boys off toward Lexington, thinking that perhaps Father George had come that far and decided to spend the night.

Eliza spent the next few hours on her knees, praying for her husband (and no doubt for herself), wondering where she had failed him and why he had chosen the path that he did.

Toward midnight she heard voices above the frog choruses in the creek and hurried out to see a procession coming out of the bush, lighting their way with lanterns. She recognized Henry Williamson and his father, from Greenville, leading the way, and instinctively she knew what they had come to tell her.

The facts were stark and harsh; there was no way to soften the blow. Father had died in the home of a lady friend in Greenville, apparently of a sudden heart attack.

In later years Speaker Williamson would recall that eery scene. "My father took my brother and myself to her mission to announce that Father George had died. We were expecting that Mother Eliza would be frustrated. All she said was, 'Let's pray.' She led us in prayer and then got up revived and strong enough to follow us to Greenville to get the body."

In Liberia's heat, with no embalming system, it was necessary to bury the corpse within 24 hours. Mother and some of the children brought the body back to Kelton in a hammock that very night and placed it in a simple coffin which had been made in a nearby village. But when she asked some of the villagers to dig a grave on the mission, they insisted that she give them their usual payment of cane juice. With her utter distaste for liquor, Mother indignantly sent them away. Taking a few of the older boys to a quiet, sheltered spot on the edge of the mission, she took her turn with them as they dug Father's grave themselves.

What did she think as she stood the next day, surrounded by her children and many friends who had come up to the mission from Greenville and Lexington to pay their last respects to the man who had brought her to Sinoe? Did she ever regret her decision? Had she ever been tempted to break the contract, which had lasted 21 years?

Never in her letters or personal conversations with her friends did she ever indicate that she had made the wrong choice. In later years she would remember only the good things—his intelligence and his musical ability.

She would love to recount the story of how he stood at the grave of Mrs. Livingston in East Africa and shed tears when he realized that this white woman had given her life to bring the gospel to his brothers and sisters in Africa. It was there that he had dedicated his life to missionary service, and that desire had brought him to Liberia.

Few of her supporters in America remember meeting Mr. George or even hearing Mother Eliza speak of him. One of the Horton brothers, in whose parents' home Mother spent so much of her time when she was in Monrovia, assessed the marriage this way:

"She was very sad about that situation. I don't think it could have worked; in the light of her character, her gifts, and her calling, it would have been difficult to have found a suitable husband. She was too absorbed in working for people to give sufficient affection, attention, and time to her husband. He would have to have been exactly like her. But husbands want to take the lead and want the wife to give them a certain amount of time. It would have been hard for her unless she had changed."

Suddenly, when the funeral was over and her worries about Father George were laid to rest, Eliza collapsed. She could see no way to stay in Africa; she felt defeated, tired, and unable to cope. Now that she was alone, she felt she could not carry on even though Father George had done very little to lighten the load during recent years.

It was now that her investment of love in the mission children came to her rescue. One of her "children" recalls that after Father died, "we prayed and fasted (she had taught us to do that). We comforted her by singing 'country songs,' civilized songs (English hymns) . . . we prayed fervently. Her heart 'came down,' and she started her work again."

In the years ahead Eliza would rest heavily upon the fellowship and help of her children, who had now grown into young men and women who loved God and wanted to serve Him.

Many of these children had grown up watching their own parents in the villages scratch the very flicker of life out of the soil, totally dependent upon their own resources. This would be Kelton's fate in the next few years as the "Hitler war" touched North Africa and closed even neutral Liberia's ports to almost all traffic. Not only did this affect the financial remittances for Mother's work, but goods imported into Liberia became scarce and prices sky high.

Over the years Mother had become more and more Liberian in her lifestyle; now she simply had to adapt to the "country ways" in times of want.

Meat was always scarce, for the tribal people had depleted the supply of game. But hunting was one of the "country ways" to fight hunger.

Somewhere along the line Mother brought a gun with her to Liberia; she knew how to shoot it, too! One of her children remembers her bringing down a hawk on the wing!

She taught some of the older boys how to use the gun, and they would go out hunting for deer or bush cows, which are a rather dangerous type of African buffalo. Large game was scarce in the area, but perhaps the most reliable source of meat was the porcupine.

Mother's attitude toward hunger and need impressed itself indelibly upon the mission children. Her faith never wavered even when God made her wait a long time for the answer. During this time of need the children frequently had to sit down to a meal of dry palm nuts. Each nut had a very small outside layer of tasteless meat, the palm nut itself being the source of palm oil.

It was perhaps in these days that Mother instituted her practice of Monday fasts. The children all knew that this was the day Mother was not to be disturbed, but also the day when she would not punish as severely as the others either.

Many times the children joined in the fasts with her, perhaps because it was preferable to another meal of palm nuts or palm cabbage (the heart of the palm leaf, near the trunk, and eaten only in times of dire need).

But that's not what the children remember. They do remember praying for $500 to cover a debt at the Dutch store in Greenville, where Mother had purchased all that the proprietor would allow on credit. The children prayed and fasted for several days, again singing a ditty to the tune of "Glory, Glory, Hallelujah." "$500 is a wise word .... to glorify our Lord."

When one of the last ships to come to Greenville in 1939 blew her siren, it was heard on the mission, and Mother and several boys hurried to the beach in great anticipation. Charles reports, "She came backs saying, 'Oh children, the money is here.' And so it was. Now she could pay her bills, but there was still nothing for us to live on."

Whether it was making soap from the native eddo root's ashes, or salt by boiling off the sea water from the drums which the boys brought from the beach, Mother looked at it as an exciting challenge and a team effort for all of them to participate. She was determined not to give in to discouragement, even when she was down to one dress to wear. When it was time to wash it, she warned the children not to come in while she dried it over the fire. The rest of her wardrobe had long since been remade into clothes for the children or given to tribal women in exchange for produce.

Many times the villagers took advantage of Mother's love and concern. They borrowed money and asked favors, knowing that she found it hard to turn them down. When the steamship whistle blew in Sinoe's port, even the village people knew Mother might be getting money, and before she or her boys were back from Greenville, they were arriving on the station carrying cassavas, plantains, peanuts, and other produce to sell to her.

Often Eliza instructed that something be purchased from each person; she wanted each one to go away with a little money, if only one or two cents.

The sheer grit of it all was summarized in a banner which she had the boys hang over the entrance to the dining room during this time: LIFTING OTHERS AS WE CLIMB.

Mother Eliza realized that the fulfillment of her dreams to send young missionaries out was drawing closer. Newspaper had recently been ordained by the Liberian Baptist Association and was preaching regularly in nearby villages. Charles and Petro were also preaching, with the hopes of being ordained soon.

She had taught them all she could, and they were ready to move on. She also sensed that strong attractions between the older boys and certain girls could no longer be denied. Marriage had already been deferred much longer here at the mission than back in the villages, where girls were given to their husbands soon after puberty.

Lu Carpenter says that Mother Eliza was concerned when she noticed that "boys and girls started loving. She said to me, 'You be good now, and don't do bad again.'"

When Lu showed an interest in one of the boys on the mission, Mother George advised, "No, don't look to that boy. You must look again. You are civilized; you must make something of yourself. Don't think that boy will go far. There are other boys here."

When Lu and Charles began to pay special attention to each other, Mother approved but with this warning, "All right, but if you are grown-up enough to love, you ought to get married."

Before Mother could help the young couples get married and then send them out to the villages (now begging for missionaries to start a church and a school), she needed more money.

Even the building situation on the mission was critical, for termites had undermined the foundations of the main mission house, and part of it had fallen in.

So once again she fell back on her only source of supply. This time she divided the children in "prayer committees," giving each little group one item to pray for:

> lumber for a substantial mission house
> zinc for roofs for buildings
> a large canoe to go to Sinoe and upstream villages
> Bibles and songbooks
> more girls
> new friends for the mission
> funds for the work at large, including new missions
> safe return of girls from America.

Whereas in 1940 only $180 came in outside of the regular support from the McAllen Baptist Church, as a result of the "prayer committeees" almost $1500 was received in the year 1942.

The main mission house was rebuilt that year, and Newspaper and Francis were married and sent to the town of Seedor, some eight miles away. The town leaders had erected a church building and were urging Mother Eliza to send a pastor. At last her first missionary couple had been launched.

chapter eighteen

Who Will Tell Me Of God?

Life was very hard for our family in the interior. Even though the tribal war was over, soldiers would still come to our village and demand that we give them our chickens or goats and other things. We couldn't afford to lose our meager supplies, but we were afraid to resist.

Though we were very poor, my mother always found ways to take care of strangers when they passed through our village. Her own mother, Dehwlo, had been known as the "Kleba Nyonnoh," or the most generous person in the village, and my mother, Nyonabe, tried to follow her example as best she could.

But I resented it whenever strangers passing through the village were invited to our house. At first mother allowed me and my two brothers to eat with the guests, but I made a pig of myself, stuffing my mouth with handfuls of rice and grabbing another handful before I could even swallow what I had. Mother was ashamed of me. She wouldn't let me eat with the guests after that. Then I would just sit and glare at the visitors, making them feel uncomfortable until they would invite me to the table. From then on mother made me sit outside the house until the guests had finished eating.

I don't know what made me so incorrigible; in fact, the whole village asked that question. "What's the matter with that son of Marwieh's?" they would ask, and my poor parents were at their wit's end.

Even though I loved my mother dearly, I found myself doing terrible things. I can remember seeing her sitting on a bench outside the house and impulsively picking up a stick to throw at her legs. I missed her and struck a child, hurting him badly.

At times like that the villagers would join my parents in meting out a punishment. That time they held me down on the ground by my legs and arms while they poured a bowl of hot pepper soup down my nose. I nearly choked to death, and for hours afterward my nose burned.

I couldn't understand myself; after one of those episodes I would go off into the forest and pound my head against a tree, crying, "What's wrong with me? I should kill myself." I hated being the "white sheep" of the family.

But one day when I was about 12 years old, a boy returned to our village from the coast, where he had been visiting his father. None of us younger ones had ever seen the ocean, so we crowded around him to hear all about it. It was as though he had been to the moon and back.

Enjoying the acclaim, he kept us spellbound with his experiences as he recounted the strange things he saw. Among other things, he told about how some people on the coast met together in a house on Sundays, and there they sang and stayed a long time. He couldn't figure out what they were doing, and finally his curiosity got the better of him, so he asked one of the villagers, "What do you do in there for such a long time?" They told him they were praying to God, who created everything, and they said they believed He heard their prayers.

I had never heard anything like this, but it excited me, and I wanted to pray to God too. I asked the boy to meet me on Sunday, and we would go someplace outside the village and he could tell me how to pray. But he wasn't interested.

Disappointed, I decided the next Sunday to try it by myself. I went to a hut that my cousin was still building, and with no one around I tried to pray for the first time. I had never heard anyone pray before, but I decided I would just talk to this God like he was my father. I can't explain what happened, but it was an exciting experience—I wanted to know more about this God, but there was no one in our village who knew anything about Him. So for two years I kept praying by myself and hoping that someday someone would come along who could tell me more.

About this time the government started building a motor road to prepare for automobiles, and I (along with most of my male relatives) spent two weeks per month for the next two years building roads under terrible working conditions.

Then I went back to Seedor, where I had been born, and stayed with my cousin. There I made the most wonderful discovery of my life, for in Seedor there was a church house, and people met together to pray to the God who created the world.

How excited I was! I could hardly wait for Sunday to come. All night I lay on my mat, waiting for the bell that my cousin said would ring to call people to church.

That morning I sat at the back of the church, listening to a preacher tell me about God for the first time in my life. I found that He was far more wonderful than I had ever imagined back in Shaw. The preacher said that God loved the world so much that He sent His only Son, Jesus, to take away my sins. I wondered if He knew how terrible I was and the awful things I had done back in my village. But the preacher said that no matter what I had done, God would forgive me and make my heart clean again.

I knew it was all true; hadn't this God heard my prayers back in Shaw when I talked to Him and asked Him to help me? Hadn't He sent me here to Seedor when I didn't even know He had one of His churches here?

I gave my heart to God that morning; it was nice to know He had a Son too—He was really a Father, just like I had been praying to Him.

The first thing I wanted to do after that was to go back home and tell my mother, Nyonabe. She would be so glad to know that her "white sheep" was a different person. And I wanted her to know that God loved her too.

Before I could go home, another wonderful thing happened to me. The preacher told me he had a school in the village, and that if I could get something to wear—he didn't allow naked children—I could come to his school.

I rushed home to tell my cousin all these good things, but he discouraged me. "You have nothing to wear, Doh, and I only have what I have on, so I can't give you anything."

But then my cousin's wife interrupted him. "Tar, he can wear my booba (blouse). I only wear it when I'm going visiting. He can bring it back to me every day after school if I need it."

Tar scoffed at that. "Who ever heard of a boy going to school in a booba? I'm sure Teacher Newspaper wouldn't allow it."

But so determined was I to go to school that I didn't mind what I wore, and I dashed over to the church house where Teacher Newspaper and his wife lived to ask him if I could come to school in a booba.

"It doesn't matter what you wear, Doh. I'll try to get a shirt from Mother Eliza for you as soon as I can, but for now the booba is just fine." Then he added, "And since you're going to be learning and getting civilized, I think you need a new name—a civilized name. I'll think about that too."

The next morning I appeared at the church house long before the bell for school rang, dressed in my cousin's white blouse, which hung to my knees. And when Newspaper introduced me to the other *children in the class, I found that he had decided on my "civilized name"—from now on I was to be Augustus Marwieh.*

Newspaper and his wife had been at Seedor for just over a year when Mother sent an urgent message that they return to Kelton. Another teacher had left, and with now over 100 children on the mission, she could not manage without Newspaper's help. And so the Georges and three of their students who were living with them—Morris Campbell, Andrew Saydee, and Augustus Marwieh—returned to Kelton.

Mother welcomed the boys warmly. She was excited to learn that Morris was already a gifted preacher and a brilliant student as he studied under Newspaper and soaked up all the knowledge he could.

Morris had a spiritual maturity and zeal for God that touched a respondent chord in Mother's heart, and she sensed that he had leadership potential she could put to use.

On the other hand, Augustus was small for his 15 years. His voluminous eyes seemed as oversized for his face as did the khaki hand-me-down shirt draped over his thin body. He gave Mother Eliza a shy smile when he was introduced to her. He had heard so much about this "God-woman" that he was tongue-tied, though he managed to stammer a Kru "thank you" for the shirt she had sent out of the mission barrel—the first piece of clothing he had ever owned.

Newspaper hastened to assure Mother that his unlikely-looking protege was a good student and would learn English quickly. In the months ahead Mother nicknamed Augustus "local preacher," for this once-tongue-tied youngster was soon preaching with the best of them.

It's not that Mother had much extra time for the new students that Newspaper had brought, for she was busy preparing for Charles and Lu's wedding.

Mother did not necessarily disapprove of the traditional dowry system of marriage practiced by the tribal people, but when her own children on the mission married, she gave them a typical Western wedding with all the trappings. Thus Charles and Lu were given royal treatment—a white dress, flowers, a huge meal for all the guests on the station, and a wedding journey to Wedjah, 40 miles inland from the coast.

Mother had been receiving requests from the chief of the Juarzon District to start a school for some time. There was only one other elementary school in the whole district, and thousands of tribal children had never had the opportunity to attend school one day of their lives. Mother had been praying about the needs in that area for some time, and now the day had come when she could send a missionary couple to start a work for God there.

Since the Sinoe River was not navigable for more than a few miles inland, the young couple traveled by foot on narrow jungle trails. Several of the younger children accompanied them, carrying the few household items that Mother had been able to accumulate for them. But no honeymoon couple ever left with more anticipation or good wishes than the Carpenters as they set off on their long trek that July afternoon in 1943.

In the midst of this fulfillment of Mother Eliza's dreams, tragedy once again struck. Instead of sending another little girl to the mission, as she had prayed, God took Leetha home. Leetha had been very special to Mother, having come to the mission when she was just a tiny baby, and in a sense replacing the loss of Cerella. Those who remember Leetha say that she was a precocious child who made a definite commitment to Christ when only five years old.

It all started with a simple throat infection, but after Mother used her usual home remedies, the hot little body continued to burn up with fever. With no doctor within 200 miles, Mother felt helpless as she watched the suffering child tossing and turning on the bed. She sat up with her night after night, bathing and soothing her, listening to her delirious prattle, trying to get her to take a few sips of water to cool her parched lips.

Toward daylight of the last day, Leetha seemed to come out of her delirium and nestled into Mother's arms as she whispered her last prayer into her ear: "Lord bless Mother Eliza, all the mission children, and me, for Jesus' sake. Amen."

Leetha was buried on the mission beside Father George that very day.

But when her family in the tribe heard of her death, the leaders came to demand reparations of $250—a Sno-country custom if a tribal member dies in an area outside his home. They believed that some evil curse had fallen upon Leetha, and since she was outside her own tribal protections, she had succumbed.

Wearily Mother allowed the older mission boys to settle the matter with the men, knowing they would know the proper procedure to follow. Reluctantly the chief and his men agreed they would not press charges and left the mission without disturbing Mother again.

But even this sorrow could not totally dampen Mother's joy in being able to at last expand her work into the interior.

By the end of 1943 there were four substations besides Kelton under Mother's supervision. Early in 1944 the pastors and leaders of the churches in these areas gathered to form the "Pleasanton Baptist Association," named in honor of the beloved Texas pastor who had so faithfully backed Mother's work over the years.

Rev. James Bolo was elected the first moderator of the association, Rev. Newspaper George became the secretary, and Rev. Charles Carpenter was the treasurer.

At 65 years of age Mother Eliza's lifelong dreams, which seemed so long in coming, were suddenly being fulfilled. Now if only the girls she had sent to the U.S.A. for training would return to help her, she was sure she could open more schools and churches in the interior, where so few had ever heard the gospel.

chapter nineteen

Retired From Duty?

When the letter arrived from the National Baptist Convention, it was as if the clock had been turned back 30 years, to the time when that other letter from another board had changed the course of her life.

Mother had been corresponding with Maude and Cerella, urging them to come back to Africa. Maude had completed her B.S. degree in Florida and had also finished a practical nurses' course at Baylor University Hospital in Texas. Cerella had completed a high school course in secretarial work. Neither of the girls was clear about her plans.

But now the letter from the Foreign Mission Board finalized everything. Dr. J.P. Reeder, the corresponding secretary of the National Baptist Convention, and Mrs. M.A.B. Fuller, the president of the Women's Missionary Union, were bringing the girls back to Africa. The Baptist officials were looking forward to seeing the work they had been supporting for so many years.

Busy days of preparations followed. (Newspaper, who by now had joined Morris in the work at Butaw, was recalled to help plan the occasion.) Mother was adept at giving a typical Liberian welcome, gathering all the dignitaries together (in this case the workers and other church leaders from the sub-missions) and preparing a lengthy program of speeches and choir numbers.

Very few of the children remembered Maude and Cerella, for it had been 13 years since they had left Liberia, but they had heard Mother praying for them so many times that they seemed like part of the family.

Mother didn't go to Monrovia to meet the party, though she did go to the capital two or three times a year if possible to take care of business and to get supplies not available in Sinoe. She had even made the heaving, 200-mile journey in an open rowboat several times, though steamers were more frequent now.

The reunion in Greenville was a time of laughing and crying, all talking at once, remembering their last trip together. Names of family and friends spilled over into the conversation—how's Mama? Is Jimmy still there? How about the Burches and the Hortons?

But she couldn't neglect Dr. Reeder and Mrs. Fuller, who on their first trip to this steamy land were looking uncomfortable and a bit apprehensive.

Eliza arranged that the guests be taken out to the mission partway by canoe. Fortunately, the mission house had been rebuilt, and by crowding the children together in one of the other huts, the guests were able to have rooms on the second floor of the mission house. How the children had scoured the plank floor and pounded and scrubbed Mother's few sheets at the river "laundry" until they were almost as white as new!

She planned that Maude and Cerella would stay with her for the time being, and then make other arrangements after the board members had gone.

The children and church workers waited at the mission most of the day in excited anticipation. Posting lookouts on the trail, they spent the day in singing and endless talking; Mother used to marvel at how the tribal people never seemed to run out of things to talk about. And of course the workers who had come together from their scattered posts clustered together, sharing their own special kind of talk as they compared problems and successes.

Village women had come in to help prepare the festive meal, and they sat around in the outdoor kitchens, occasionally stoking their open fires under the simmering kettles or lifting the lid to check the progress.

Children scampered in and out of the crowds, playing the inevitable tag, or teasing the one in their group who was the brunt of their displaced humor. Babies were jostled on little sisters' backs until they began to howl; then they were quickly transferred to the warm, brown dinner bars offered by their mothers, and their sisters were free to scamper away and join the fun.

Knowing that Mother disapproved of nakedness, even the village women wore some kind of colorful cloth over their breasts, and their bright, hand-woven lappas (wraparound skirts) were matched by head-scarves tied in a variety of imaginative ways.

When the party was at last spotted down the trail, the people surged forward, singing and clapping and performing little dance steps of welcome, accompanying the tired travelers into the thatched church.

One after another of Mother's "children" gave a speech, thanking the visitors for their help over the years and welcoming the two girls warmly. Deacons and women's leaders from the substations spoke in their native dialects, interpreted by Newspaper, who acted as the master of ceremony. A dozen choirs shared in the program, their drums beating a persistent accompaniment, with the offbeat clapping adding to the African rhythm.

Listening to the beautiful harmonies and throbbing rhythms, the visitors from the deep South of the U.S. must have felt right at home.

After each of the women guests was presented with a colorfully woven "lappa," which was the traditional women's dress in the villages, Dr. Reeder was bedecked in a handwoven chief's robe. Already sweltering in his traditional dark suit and tie, it must have taken an effort of great will for Dr. Reeder to thank the donors. He certainly couldn't have known the tremendous sacrifice this gift represented!

When the excitement died down, and the people returned to their homes, Mother and Dr. Reeder, Mrs. Fuller, and Maude began their discussions. It was not clear to Mother exactly what they had in mind, though she sensed that they were holding something back from her.

Mrs. Fuller was insistent that Mother come home for a rest. "You've been here for ten years, Mother, without a vacation of any kind. Maude and Cerella are here now to help you, and this is a good time for you to come back."

Mother finally agreed to their persistence, though she had hoped to stay and help Maude get started on the work. Cerella was to begin doing the secretarial work and perhaps teach some of the girls how to type and keep simple books. But she conceded that it might be better to take a break first, and let the girls just keep the station going for now.

But Dr. Reeder's second suggestion met with Mother's adamant refusal. It seemed they felt the mission was too difficult to reach—off the road, far from town. Dr. Reeder finally came out with his plan. "We would like to move the work to Monrovia, where it will be closer to the center of activity and easier to maintain communications."

Mother was aghast! There were dozens of churches in Monrovia. And what about the native children, who were not welcome in civilized society yet? Where would they go to school? Who would spread the gospel to the tribes in the hinterland, who had never even once had a missionary come and tell them about Christ?

"Why, Dr. Reeder, when I visit some of those tribes and tell them that Jesus died for them, they ask me, 'Why haven't you come before to tell us about Him?' "

Desperate, Mother sent word for Newspaper to come back to the station to help defend her position. After days of discussions, Dr. Reeder finally agreed that, rather than going to Monrovia, they would move the mission a few miles south to the motor road being built in anticipation of automobiles being brought into the country. In fact, the very first auto had been introduced into Sinoe Country only recently!

Concerned for the future of her beloved substations (which were far more isolated than Kelton was), Mother urged Dr. Reeder and Mrs. Fuller to visit at least one, the most accessible being Butaw, where Newspaper had gone several months earlier to help Morris Campbell. The work there had grown so fast that Mother felt it warranted another missionary. Augustus Marwieh had gone along with his teacher.

Gus says today, "I well remember the frantic preparations that we made on the station and how we practiced saying, 'How do you do, Dr. Reeder.' "

Before the officials of the Foreign Mission Board left Liberia, they acquired a 1000-acre site along the motor road for the "new Kelton" which would now be named after the National Baptist Convention. They also acquired deeds to the property of the thatched-and-mud edifice of the Morning Star Baptist Church in Butaw.

Then Mother bid her tearful and fearful goodbyes to Maude and Cerella and the rest of her children, and began her unwilling journey home.

A day out to sea from Monrovia, Dr. Reeder finally revealed everything to a shocked and heartbroken Mother George.

His message went something like this—

"Mother, you have done a heroic and commendable work in Liberia, but we have felt for some time that you were getting too old to continue directing the mission. When Maude came to us offering her services as a missionary in Liberia, she came with fine credentials. You can be very proud of that young lady, coming from the background she has, and today with a bachelor's degree.

"But Maude felt that it would be very difficult to work under you, especially since she has been well-educated and has new ideas. She was also concerned about you. You have labored in Africa for 32 years, under very difficult conditions. You've had malaria over and over; the ulcers on your legs from walking in those swamps never seem to heal. Surely God is satisfied with your long years of service, too.

"Therefore, Mother, we have decided to retire you. You can continue going around to churches to raise support for the work, and we will send it out to Maude. But we will not agree to sending you back to Kelton again."

Mother sat in stunned silence. She ventured one burning question: "Will you also be responsible for my substations?"

Dr. Reeder had some very strong opinions on this too, but he tried to be gentle. "Well, Mother, we feel you may have extended yourself too far. The work at Kelton needed every bit of money and attention you could give it; instead, you have sent your best leaders out into the interior, thus also taking financial support from the school. We feel you should have concentrated on developing a strong school, and that's what we're going to do."

Mother looked as though she had been slapped in the face.

"However," he added hastily, "since we have registered the Butaw work in the name of the National Baptist Convention, we will continue to support the work of Brother George there."

God gave Mother the grace to say quietly and sweetly, "All right, Dr. Reeder; I'll retire."

Years later Mrs. Rose Chandler Jones, who went with her husband to serve at the "new Kelton" in 1952, described what they found:

"There was nothing there. Rev. Davis, Cecelia's husband, had already taken sick and left, and the mission house was used for a way station. Passersby would go in and warm up, building a fire in the middle of the plank floor. They scorched the floors, and, well, they just ran the place down . . . . It had been empty for a year because Mr. Davis got malaria. Maude had died in 1947, and the place was in debt. She had taken a lot of money to appease the people, but she just couldn't run the mission.

When we got there, it was in a rundown condition with nothing going on. There wasn't even a church."

And in her autobiography Mother simply reported the action of the board in these words: "In 1945 the Foreign Mission Board of the National Baptist Convention of America saw fit to discontinue my services as a missionary."

Though Mother acquiesced to being retired, inwardly she was not at all sure this was God's direction. As she reminded herself, "The Convention didn't call me; God Almighty called me."

For a time she rested at home with her sisters Jenny Belle and Ellen. Papa had died some years earlier, and the little house in Taylor seemed strangely empty.

Mother waited anxiously for word from Africa, and when Newspaper's first letter arrived, her worst fears were confirmed. The Convention had written him that they had retired Mother Eliza, and they would no longer be supporting the sub-missions. If the workers wishes to receive a stipend, they would have to return to work at Kelton. Morris Campbell had already joined forces with Maude, but the other "children" were determined to man their stations as long as they could.

This word was all that Mother Eliza needed to seal her decision—she would return to Africa to work "by faith." After all, isn't that what she had been doing most of the 32 years she had been there?

She began writing letters furiously, and before long had a heavy schedule of meetings booked which took her through Texas and into California, where some of the Baptist churches had begun to take an interest in her work. One of her friends from Texas, Mrs. Elle Mae Gibbs, was now in Oakland, California, and invited her to use her home as long as she stayed in the area.

That was to begin a close relationship of many years, with Mother making Elle Mae's home her headquarters. Through Elle Mae's eyes the Mother Eliza of deputation times emerges. Mrs. Rundle, for that is Elle Mae's name today, remembers:

"I invited her to come and stay with me .... Every time she came back to California she would stay in my home. At that time the Baptists had put her down; they were not going to support her anymore. I believe the men in the denomination didn't want to send her .... They didn't think a woman was capable of staying there under the conditions she had to live under.

"I suppose Mother didn't want to relinquish her authority over what she had built up over the years, and you couldn't blame her for that."

As everyone who had Mother Eliza in her home during her travels would concur, she was a delightful person to have around. She had a sparkling sense of humor and the ability to keep herself entertained without making demands on her hostess.

Her prayer life was a constant source of wonderment to the people with whom she stayed.

Mrs. Rundells recalls, "I had a two-bedroom house; the bedrooms were across the hall from each other. I remember waking up in the middle of the night hearing Mother Eliza praying. Sometimes it would go on for an hour or more. I would drop off to sleep and wake up, and she would still be praying. The next morning she would ask, 'Honey, did I disturb you last night?' She would sometimes pray almost all night, so burdened was she for the work in Africa and the people she had left behind."

Thus it was that her sacrificial life and sweet spirit had won her many friends, and now that the mission had retired her against her wishes, these friends came to her aid.

One day while Mother was staying at her house, Elle Mae asked, "How would you like me to organize a club to help support you?"

And that was the beginning of several ELIZA DAVIS GEORGE CLUBS, who sent gifts of food and clothing over the next ten years. The Oakland, California, club, which frequently met in the home of Mrs. Madie Monroe, was the most active.

Mrs. Channel, a member of that group, remembers that there were about 15 women in the club. She rather sorrowfully commented, "So many of our people are not interested in foreign missions. They think we have enough to do at home—that Africa is such a wealthy country."

But with the backing of this club and an active group of women in Houston, Texas, plus several old faithful churches, Mother felt confident that she had a strong enough support base to return to Africa.

She persuaded Cecelia to go back to help with the work while she was raising funds. Cecelia had been longing to return to Africa for some time; her own natural mother was ill, and she wanted to see her again before she died.

Though Mr. Davis also felt called to Africa as a missionary, he did not yet have any Bible training. Furthermore, he didn't feel it was wise to go out under Mother's supervision when she was not connected with any official organization. The National

Baptist Convention agreed to send him, but only after he had taken several years of additional training.

So in 1946 Cecelia and the three children left without him with the understanding that when he had completed his Bible training he would follow them to Liberia.

Cecelia shared Mother's burden for her lost people, but there is no doubt that she also carried a load of guilt, knowing that Mother had brought her to the United States to be trained to go back to Africa. So, though it was difficult to leave her husband and face the uncertainties of life in the interior with the little children, far from medical care or easy communications, this was the lesser of two evils.

Cecelia recalls that Liberia was "a new world"—far different from her memories as a child. In 14 years of life in the West she had forgotten that there were no conveniences in the bush. Stationed at first in Butaw, where Newspaper George and his wife had a little school, Cecelia recounts:

"We were ten miles from Greenville and the nearest stores; I had to get used to using kerosene or palm-oil lamps, cutting wood for cooking, and carrying buckets of water."

Later they moved even farther inland, to Plahn, taking the boarding children with them and opening a school in the primitive village where the elderly James Bolo was pastoring a church. Now they were 25 miles from the coast, and Cecelia remembers "walking everywhere, carrying loads on my head."

In Plahn they were given a plot of ground to start the school, and they built a hut "like everyone else's, dirt floor and all." Cecelia quickly relearned how to plant a Liberian farm—rice, cassavas, a pepper patch, and vegetables—for there was little money coming from Mother Eliza.

During the rainy season, when they could not live off the garden, "there were times when we didn't have anything. We would use the last little pint of rice for breakfast, asking the Lord to send us something for dinner. And He always did; somebody would come by and say they came along to see their child and brought a little rice. The parents appreciated so much what we were doing, for there was no other school at all in the district.

"We didn't have Bibles or books. We just used old magazines to train the children to read. I had to use an interpreter, but Newspaper carried on the ministerial part; he was a good minister."

Cecelia had left her three children with Sister Maude at "new Kelton" when they moved the mission to the Plahn area, and from time to time she would make the long trek back through the jungle to visit them.

On one such visit in 1947 she felt the strangest premonitions, as she walked along, that she should have brought her black dress. As she neared the turnoff to Butaw, a man came along who recognized her and gave her a letter which he had been instructed to carry to Plahn. Opening the letter, her premonition began to take shape—Maude was very ill in the government hospital in Greenville.

The accounts of Maude's final illness are not clear. Some say she was poisoned; Cecelia says she had a burst appendix. But she also describes her symptoms: "She couldn't drink because when we carried a cup to her mouth, her jaw would lock."

Maude had been back in Africa barely two years when she died in Cecelia's and Cerella's arms while the terrified nurse fled from the room.

After Maude's death Cerella married one of the men from Greenville, where she had started working in the first branch bank in Sinoe County, no longer interested in carrying on Mother's work. Within another three years Cecelia would have to return to the U.S. with her sick husband, who had come to Liberia and succumbed to its fevers. None of the three girls in whom Mother had pinned her hopes for her work had been able to fulfill her dreams, and so she had to look elsewhere for someone to carry on her work.

chapter twenty

Big Plans

Mother Eliza's arrival in Plahn on a rainy day in October, 1948, seemed like a mirage to Newspaper and Cecelia. Mother did not depend on the haphazard communication system of the country, and usually simply arrived unannounced.

One of the Horton brothers told how they would see Mother Eliza coming down the road toward their house in Monrovia, having just gotten off the ship. "We thought she had retired several times, but there she was again. In later years she would appear in a taxi, and Mama Horton would yell out, 'There's Mother Eliza!' We would all run out and kiss her and welcome her. In the evening, after supper, she would braid Mama's hair, and we would all sit around listening to her experiences."

This time when she stopped at the Hortons on her way through Monrovia she recounted how she almost didn't make it back to Liberia. "Why, dearie (she always called Ora that), I went to the shipping company in New Orleans to book my passage, and would you believe it, they told me I was too old to travel by ship! Why, I'm only 69, I told them, but they wouldn't sell me a ticket."

Reaching over to get another candy out of the dish, which Ora had placed within easy reach (knowing her weakness for sweets), she went on: "I thought to myself, that won't stop me. I went to the airport and asked how old a person had to be to fly. They told me there's no age limit. 'As long as you got the money, you fly.' So I got on that plane and came right to Africa where I'm supposed to be, cause I'm determined that my bones will bleach on African soil."

But now, back in the interior village of Plahn after a 20-mile hike through the jungle, Mother must have surveyed her new mission with frustration. After all the years of hard work and persistent pioneering at Kelton, she was starting all over again.

The school which Newspaper and Cecelia had started was meeting in a brush arbor, the sapling framework covered with a thatch of palm leaves—hardly durable enough to last through the rainy season, thought Mother.

A little two-room, mud-and-thatch hut served as a home for the Georges and Cecelia and the few boarding children. Mother was glad to see that Augustus was still with Newspaper, and was now a bright-eyed young man who, according to Newspaper, was a brilliant student.

Otto Klebo came to welcome her too. He was living in his home village of Plandibalibo, about ten miles away, where he had also started a church. The workers told Mother proudly that the two little missions were formed into an association called the Elizabeth Native Interior Mission (ENI), which also included the sub-mission at Wedjah.

Mother could not keep back the tears as she surveyed her faithful children—Otto, Petro, Newspaper, James Bolo, Cecelia, Phillip Sota, and Charles and Lu at Wedjah. All of them would still be primitive, unevangelized "country people" if God had not brought her to train them and teach them about Him. Only Cecelia had had the privilege of advanced training. Maybe if God permitted her another ten years, there could be other native children trained as pastors and teachers, and somewhere there was one who could take her place.

At their first discussion over the future of the work, Mother announced to the workers that she would take a boy to America the next time she went back. "No more girls," she stated firmly. She was thinking about taking Andrew Saydee, who had been one of the promising students at Kelton, but the others desisted. They were unanimous in their agreement that Augustus Marwieh would be a better student and would be more likely to make a good leader.

Mother agreed to observe him more closely while she was at Plahn, and if he was indeed all they said he was, she would take him back with her the following year. For the moment she suggested that they not tell him anything about the plan.

One day Mother asked Augustus to walk along to a nearby village to hold a service. As they were walking back to the mission, Mother decided the time had come to broach the subject of going to America. She had been watching him carefully for many months, and she fully agreed that he was the most likely of all her students to succeed.

"Gustus, perhaps you know that I've been thinking about taking a boy to America to get trained so he can come back to serve his people."

Gus's heart jumped to his throat; he had heard some talk that Mother wanted to take Andrew, but his own heart had told him that would not be so.

"So, Gustus, the other recommended that I take you. They said you were clever and would make a fine leader. I've been watching and praying, son, and I believe the time has come for you to make plans to go to America with me."

Make plans! Gus had been dreaming and praying about this moment for more than four years. He had (according to his own words) "absolute confidence that God would let me go to America." Everywhere he had gone, whether to Butaw, Kelton, and now Plahn, he had found a "praying ground" to remind God of such promises as "ask and ye shall receive." He had prayed that he would be allowed to go to study in America. But no one—not even Mother Eliza or Newspaper—knew what he had been praying about.

When asked in later years how a native boy from the hinterland of Liberia would develop such an ambition, he could only respond, "from God." His was not a dream of wealth or power or even prestige, but a God-given desire to study so that he could serve among his own people.

He couldn't articulate these longings to Mother on that day in late 1948, but it was as if she could read his heart, and the same divine spark that had sent him to the "praying ground" now drove her to do everything she could to get him overseas.

For six months Mother trudged from the offices of the American consulate to the post office to the Liberian government offices, speaking to every official of any influence in Monrovia, seeking permission for Gus to go to the United States with her.

But though he was 20 years old, Gus had only completed the fifth grade, and the United States would not issue a student visa unless he was a high-school graduate. Mother then tried to obtain an immigrant's visa for him, but failed in that as well, and finally had to concede that she could not take him back to the United States this time. Leaving him in the loving and capable care of the Horton family while he attended school, Mother returned once again to America to raise more funds for her struggling ENI mission in the interior.

When she returned a year later, the picture couldn't have been bleaker: the little thatch schoolhouse at Plahn had burned down, most of the children had gone back home, and Newspaper had left the work. At 71 years of age there was nowhere to go but up.

chapter twenty one

The "Cursed" Place

Otto chopped the overhanging vine blocking their way so that Mother could follow him through the thick underbrush. They had left the narrow path several miles back and were now in totally uninhabited territory, though it was only five or six miles from Otto's home village of Plandibalibo.

When the villagers had heard where Otto was taking Mother, they had urged her not to go. "Mother, you shouldn't pass that way—that's the devil bush. One man went there one day and tried to make a farm, and after three days he just died, and nobody knows how he died. Mother Eliza, you shouldn't go."

But Mother simply reassured them, "We'll be all right, children. Don't worry, God will protect us."

As she and Otto walked away into the forest she could hear them muttering about her "strong medicine."

"They don't know that my strong medicine is the Lord, do they, Otto? Maybe someday they will learn to trust Him rather than the ju-jus they hang above their houses to protect them."

Mother and Otto walked in silence for several minutes. Only the swish of Otto's cutlass as he cleared a path or the buzz of the flies around their heads broke the hot silence.

As she walked Mother prayed, "Lord, let this be the right place; you know I don't have much more time to build a lasting work for you."

Mother had decided, in consultation with the other workers, to leave Plahn even though she had already rebuilt the thatch schoolhouse that had burned down. The government was beginning to place teachers in interior villages here and there (very few in respect to the population), but they had sent J.D. Sah-nyenneh to Plahn. When Sah-nyenneh began complaining that the children chose to go to Mother's school rather than his, she determined to move on.

"Liberia is too big and schools are too few for us to quarrel about the children in this village. I'll just go further into the interior, where there are no schools."

And so this morning in 1950 Otto was leading her to a "cursed place"—an area in Seekon district that no villager would farm because he feared the consequences. As they neared the spot, the ground began to rise slightly, so that when Otto said "This is it" they were standing on the heavily forested crest of a small knoll, with virgin jungle spread out before them and a murky creek pulsing over submerged logs along the bottom of the knoll.

Otto asked once more, "Mother, are you sure you want to build a mission on this land?"

And Mother's confident reply was, "Son, there is no place where God has told us not to stay. This is going to be my life's work. We're not going to move anywhere else."

And standing there on the little knoll, with only the birds and insects as witnesses, Mother Eliza dedicated the land that was to become a lasting monument to God's grace and her persistence in Liberia.

It seemed as though God gave her a renewed vigor to face the building of yet another mission. She purchased cutlasses, axes, and other tools, and she hired men to cut the bush and dig out the stumps of centuries-old trees, burning the brush until an area on the knoll was cleared.

Philip Sota describes the first building: "The walls were made of mud. We put sticks on the ground and tied the sticks together, then put mud on the sticks inside and out, then white chalk on the outside. We covered the roof with a special thatch from the swamp."

Leona George, one of the few girls who had followed the Georges to Plahn, recalls that "we used to work hard while we were opening the mission. Mother would teach us in the mornings, and in the afternoons we worked in the gardens."

Mother knew how essential it was to start growing rice and cassavas immediately, and so she would work out in the burning sun, bending from her waist down to "scratch rice" like every other Liberian country woman.

But the work was too hard for a 72-year-old woman. Otto recalls, "That old lady suffered. Sometimes she walked from six to six from here to Greenville. Sometimes I had to take her water and wash her feet in the night, rubbing them with alcohol, and she would say, 'Son, you have to pray about my going back home.'"

In the Seekon area Mother once again was able to visit native villages where Christ had never been named. In one village when she had told the people that she had come from across the sea, one of the old grandmothers placed her hand beside Mother's and said, "Mammy, your hand looks just like my hand. You are my sister. They said long years ago that some of our people here took our brothers away across the water. We have been looking for our brothers to come back home. You are one of our sisters that has come back to us."

Mother Eliza couldn't explain to these simple people that she firmly believed that God had allowed her brothers and sisters to be taken away as slaves so that she, like Joseph, could be used to bring salvation to her own people.

In spite of her own painful ulcers, which never seemed to leave, Mother traveled to villages with Otto or Petro to dress wounds and treat illnesses with simple medicines. Many people were converted in those village ministries. As Otto says, "They believed that God sent this missionary to them to help them, and she wasn't even from their own family!"

By 1952 there were 30 children on the mission, nearly half of them girls, to Mother's great delight. Otto's young sister-in-law, Otheliah, had moved out to ENI with her when the mission house was completed, and Mother seemed to have a special love for her. Otheliah had a gentle way of ministering to Mother's needs, brushing and platting her hair at night and keeping her room (which she still shared with the girls) neat and tidy, the way Mother liked it.

Otheliah would be the first to admit that Mother's material possessions were so few and simple that they were easy to care for. An inventory of Mother's personal belongings would have read something like this:

2 or 3 rattan chairs
a battered suitcase
a single bed, 2 sheets, 1 pillow
1 small table
1 blanket
2 or 3 dresses and other personal clothing
1 pair of sandals, 1 pair of high rubber boots
a bowl, several glasses
a face pan

1 tablecloth
1 calendar on the wall
1 bamboo mat on the floor
a big tub over an outside fire
2 or 3 kerosene lamps or a palm-oil lamp in a tin
a pressing iron for the girls' hair
a Bible
writing materials
a sun helmet

Mother never seemed to have any use for money for herself. One of her "boys" explained it this way: "She used to spend money as if she didn't need it. We've seen a lot of missionaries, but I'm still wondering if I will ever see another missionary like her. She would pray for the money. She would tell us, 'Let's pray; the mission is out of money' . . . but when the money would come in you would see the people pour in to her saying, 'Mother, I don't have this or I need that' . . . . On payday she would be completely broke; then we would go into another prayer meeting until finally somebody would provide.

"She used to give freely no matter what the problem was . . . she didn't care whether you committed a crime and needed help or whether you needed the money for religious purposes—she would give the money."

No doubt money was "wasted" through her generous, giving spirit. But many of her children remember that her generosity changed the direction of their lives.

Madie Monroe (who was named after her benefactor in California) is the matron of the girls' dormitory at ENI today. But Madie recalls that her father would not allow her to move to ENI when the mission house was ready for occupancy because he had already "dowried" her to an old man with several other wives. Madie was only about ten years old at the time, so she was still too young to join her elderly husband.

When Mother learned of this, she called Madie's father to the mission and asked how much dowry he had been paid. It was only $15, but Mother gave him $40 so that the man could not give an argument later that he had been cheated.

It wasn't as if Mother didn't concern herself about money. Mr. Miller, a neighbor near Kelton, once met her in Greenville during these early ENI days. She seemed unusually dispirited when he stopped to talk to her. "Oh, Mr. Miller, I came to town because I thought there would be some money, but there is nothing. I'm afraid I'm really down."

Rather surprised at this unusual admission of defeat from this stouthearted missionary, Mr. Miller asked, "You mean you're giving up and going back to the States?"

"Oh, no," she retorted, "I'll endure. I'll stay until I've established this mission." And, throwing back her shoulders, she shifted her walking stick and continued up the road, fully restored from her momentary despondency.

But, at 72, the long walks were really getting too much for Mother. The ulcers on her legs would not heal, and she would walk with a stick, hopping along to keep the weight off her sore leg. She never complained, and if she thought people were looking, she would try to ignore the pain and walk as normally as possible.

Someone suggested that she should get a jeep to get her back and forth into the mission. Taken up by the idea, she wrote to her faithful clubs and churches about the need. It was an exciting day at the mission when a letter came saying that enough funds had been provided through her faithful prayers, and with the help of the Lincoln Hatchery in Lincoln, Nebraska, a jeep was on its way. It would be some months yet before it arrived, but Mother talked of nothing else than being able to drive to town for supplies or to take the children to high school in town. The fact that she had never driven anything in her life never daunted her for a minute!

chapter twenty two

Son, Let's Pray

In 1944, William Vacanarat Shadrach Tubman became the nineteenth president of the Republic of Liberia. He was to serve the better part of seven terms, and he brought stability and unification of the tribal groups to the country.

As a Christian leader, Tubman was interested in missionary work, and the contributions of Mother Eliza in Sinoe soon came to his attention. It was under his administration that Mother's school first received a small monthly stipend.

Having lost BIA in Fortesville, the Kelton Mission, and the Plahn substation to the vacillations of overseas mission boards, Mother determined that it would never happen again. Approaching President Tubman, who had given her an audience and sympathetic hearing on various occasions, Mother presented a petition for a grant of land in the Seekon territory where she had begun building ENI mission. In 1952 Tubman granted her 500 acres with the promise that it was hers to use as long as she lived.

Though some of the older workers from Kelton days were faithfully serving with her, Mother Eliza was fully aware that none of them were qualified to develop ENI into a far-reaching work.

Her heart was still determined to send Augustus overseas. The reports she was receiving about his progress in Monrovia were encouraging. Though he had only completed five years of schooling in the bush, Mrs. Horton had persuaded him to take the eighth-grade entrance examination, which he had passed with flying colors. After a few weeks it became obvious to the perceptive Mama Horton that even the eighth-grade work was not challenging him, for every quiz he brought home was a near-perfect paper.

Ora wrote a note to her dear friend in the interior, telling her that she had gone to the dean himself when Gus's shyness prevented him from speaking for himself. And the dean recognized immediately that this young man was brilliant and self-taught and should be put up another grade. Now in his third year in the high-school division of Liberia College, Gus was still at the top of his class.

But Mother was more concerned about his spiritual growth and his burden for his own people. Many of her friends were trying to dissuade her from sending Gus to the U.S., reminding her of the disappointment which the girls had been.

One friend in whom she had a lot of confidence summarized the situation. "He's just a young man, Mother. When he gets over there, he'll meet all kinds of nice American girls, and he won't want to come back and marry some country girl who's not had the education and experiences he's had. He'll just end up staying there. And even if he does come back, would he fit with his people in the bush? Did Maude fit after her American education? No, she felt above them and could never really identify with her own people again. It's just too big a risk, Mother."

Mother knew there was a lot of truth in what her friends were telling her. But on the other hand, she knew that to provide the leadership which would bring the people out of their centuries of ignorance and isolation, it would take a man trained beyond what Liberia's present educational system could provide. There was no theological school of higher training in Liberia that could give Gus the challenge his responsive mind and visionary heart needed.

So Mother continued to wrestle with God about this perplexing question, knowing that she could trust God if it was His will, but not really sure whether it was.

And so it was that when Gus was suddenly called back to the interior for the funeral of his brother, Mother felt she had to spend some time with him. She had been planning to visit the Carpenters in Wedjah, and since she never walked those long stretches through the bush alone anymore, it was an ideal time to ask Gus to accompany her.

While I was in Shaw for my brother's funeral, Mother sent a message for me to come to the mission, which was ironically now only 20 minutes' walk from my home. She wanted to pray with me and comfort me in my loss.

When I got to ENI I was surprised at the development in such a short time. Though the buildings were still of thatch and mud, they were larger than in Plahn and neatly spaced on either side of the knoll. Mother asked me to teach a few classes while I was there, and I was impressed with the bright students that had come to study at ENI.

Then Mother asked if I would take a journey with her—first to Greenville, where she had some business to do, and then back through Wedjah to visit the Carpenters. She felt responsible to visit their work and encourage them from time to time, and she had not been there for a long while.

That walk with Mother was a turning point in my life. We had hours, just the two of us, to open our hearts and share our innermost needs.

Mother told me of some of the experiences she had in Kelton, things I had never known before. She talked about the people around the mission who had come to know Christ, and other villages she had never been able to visit because of the press of time and work.

Remembering those people, Mother stopped and, putting her hand on my shoulder as we stood in the burning sun, she said, "Son, let's pray." And then she poured her heart out to the Lord for Maneytown and Murraysville, for the families she knew and the children she had raised, weeping copiously as she prayed.

Then we moved on, Mother leading the way with that tall walking stick which had by now become almost as much of a trademark as her pith helmet. "Son, all these 40 years in Africa I've been crying over the lost. Who's going to tell them that Jesus loves them and died for them? Who is going to free them from their ju-ju and devil dancers? Who's going to educate those precious baby girls and keep them from being sold to old men who are just looking for another slave to work in the garden?"

"Son, let's pray." This time she knelt on the trail, her face lifted to the sun, its light reflecting off her thick glasses, which she had been wearing since her last visit to the States.

Sometimes she asked me to pray. Then again she stopped suddenly in her tracks and said, "You know, son, God has something special in mind for you. He's given you a good mind—yes, a good mind—and He wants you to use it for Him. But, son, don't forget your people here in Seekon, and all those in the interior without Christ. Commit your life to serve Him here among your own people; don't ever disobey His call.

"Son, let's pray...."

And so we walked and talked and stopped and prayed—walk, talk, stop, pray.

On the way back from Lexington, we left at eleven in the morning, not arriving at Wedjah until two a.m. She never seemed to get tired; she never stopped teaching. It was as if she was pouring her life's desires into me until they were pressed down and running over.

As it grew dark, I began to worry about Mother; the road was very rough, with twisted roots reaching out into the path, vines catching us, and branches slapping us across the face.

That night I counted that Mother fell down five times. It looked like somebody had lifted her feet up from under her as she flew sprawling into the bush. I was frightened, but as I helped pick her up and brush her off, she would quote a verse that had become descriptive of her

African walks: "For a just man falleth seven times and riseth up again" (Proverbs 24:16).

The next morning, when I got out of bed at the Carpenter's place, I was still tired and sore, and I hobbled to the door. I couldn't believe my eyes to find Mother Eliza singing merrily and sweeping the veranda! She was none the worse for wear after her 15-mile walk the day before!

In fact, Mother hardly gave her falls another thought—the walk had given her the final assurance that Gus was the man of God's choice to send overseas for training so that he could take over her work. God had spared her life through so many falls and dangers that He could surely keep her for the next seven or eight years while Gus completed his education. What were a few scratches or ulcers and a few more bouts of malaria if in the end God would open up the interior of Liberia for the gospel?

With Gus in his final year of high school, Mother realized that she would have to raise the passage money for Gus to go to the U.S.A. One day an idea came to her that she hoped would mean she would not have to burden her faithful "clubs" with yet another project. R.G. Le Tourneau of the U.S. had begun an ambitious project in the Baffu Bay area, some 60 miles from ENI. She had heard he had brought a lot of heavy equipment to clear the forest and develop the land, and that he had a ship of his own to bring materials and personnel back and forth. Perhaps he could take Gus to the U.S. on his ship.

With her usual impetuosity, Mother decided to go and see Le Tourneau herself. Taking Otheliah, they walked to the main road and were able to catch a ride on a truck to Greenville.

The stopover in Greenville was especially pleasant, since Senator Mitchell had completed his big new house. Elizabeth Mitchell was the principal of the demonstration school in Greenville and was a warmhearted person who felt that she should help Mother in her sacrificial ministry. Though she had been sending meals to Mother whenever she learned she was staying in town, she had promised that when her new house was completed, Mother would have her own comfortable "prophet's chamber." Sure as her word, when the house was completed, she turned a key over to Mother so that she could come and go without feeling she was disturbing anyone.

Mrs. Mitchell did complain about one thing, however. "If her girls came down with her, she wouldn't ask for another room. She would sleep on the floor and put them in her bed. I didn't know this until I happened to walk in the room one time and see the two girls in the bed, Mother on the floor. I took her upstairs and gave her my room.

"Mother felt uneasy. 'Daughter, I don't want to embarrass you.'"

But Mrs. Mitchell assured her, "I want to do this. You are doing for me what I am not willing to do myself. Why couldn't I have gone out there to work? Just accept this as my contribution."

So for ten years, whenever Mother came into Greenville she had a comfortable room at her disposal and nourishing food prepared.

On this particular day in 1953, Mother and Otheliah woke very early, for they had a 25-mile walk along the beach ahead of them. Mother remembered the heat and the tortuous struggle of her walk some 23 years earlier, and she urged Otheliah that they get a head start on the sun.

This was Otheliah's baptism into walking on the beach, and she still marvels, "I don't see how she lived through that walk to Monrovia. Even with shoes on, the sand was so hot. Mother wore canvas shoes, and she walked on the edge of the beach where the swell would come to cool her feet."

They arrived at Baffu Bay late Saturday night and bedded down in a friendly village. (Praise God for the wonderful way the natives treat strangers in their midst, Mother would often say.) Cleaning themselves up as best they could, they arrived at the mission station in time for church. After the service they were introduced to Le Tourneau, who invited them for dinner.

But the news was not good. Yes, one ship had come with the equipment and personnel for the project, but it had already gone back, and they were not planning on taking the equipment back, so there was no need of another ship.

Mother understood and thanked Le Tourneau for his invitation for dinner. Getting up from the table, she whispered to Otheliah, "Come, let's go, daughter. It's time we started for home."

Otheliah still remembers the pain in her feet. "I just felt like crying. I was so tired, and here she was, 74 years old and ready to turn right around and walk back again."

But Le Tourneau read Mother's intentions and told her to wait. In a few minutes he had sent word to one of the pilots on the station, and Mother and Otheliah were bundled into the plane for the ten-minute flight back to Greenville. When Mother demurred at "embarrassing him," he shook his head. "Nonsense, Mother Eliza—I wouldn't think of letting you walk back that distance again. I'm only sorry I couldn't help you with the young man you want to send overseas."

Le Tourneau couldn't help Mother then, but years later Mother's "young man" would shoulder the whole responsibility of the churches which had grown out of this ill-fated Baffu Bay project.

chapter twenty three

The Jeep and the Journey

The jeep whined in lowest gear as it struggled to inch forward through the underbrush. Farther down the path Otto and several of the workmen continued to chop at a stump that was the last obstacle before crossing the creek ahead.

The jeep had arrived at Sinoe port a week before, and with great jubilation Mother and the older boys had gone to collect it. When the ship's crane deposited it on the dock, it seemed as though hundreds of children converged on it, swarming all over to get a good look at this strange vehicle. In 1953 a new car in the county was still an oddity!

Mother had the foresight to have one of the government drivers come to the dock with her to show her how to operate the levers and buttons. She did not doubt for a minute that with a few simple instructions she could drive the jeep safely home.

Of course, there was the problem of getting the jeep to the station once they reached the end of the dirt motor road, since there was another 12 miles of uncharted jungle and swamp before they reached the mission. As soon as she had heard that the jeep was on its way, Mother began badgering the county to send a crew to build a road to ENI. Roads were still built by the porter system—one shovel of dirt at a time, carried by one man at a time—and it was a slow task. But though there had been many promises, there was no sign of a road to ENI yet (and wouldn't be for another 15 years). Mother was determined to get the jeep to the mission somehow.

With her indomitable spirit she managed to drive the jeep as far as Plahn the first day, where the dirt road ended. No doubt she gave her passengers some unexpected thrills with her erratic steering and her sudden spurts on the gas or her slammed brakes; but they took it with the same good humor she did. She hadn't had so much fun in years! Posing to have her picture taken on main street with her boys and some of her friends standing proudly behind the vehicle, she looked as though she had been doing this all her life.

But now out in the jungle the fun seemed to have gone out of the venture. Revving the engine to a high whine, she charged into a creek whose fast-flowing waters threatened to carry the jeep away. The wheels spun in a mudhole while Otto and the others rhythmically heaved and released to rock them out of the mud. The horseflies buzzed incessantly around their perspiring bodies, adding to the tortures of heat, mosquitoes, and burns of branches scraping their arms and foreheads as they pushed through the brush.

But though it took almost 24 hours for the last 12 miles, Mother *did* get the jeep home, to the cheers of the waiting children and their teachers. Otto maintains that he kept the jeep road open through the brush with his cutlass and shovel for more than a year. No one seems to know where the gasoline came from there in the interior or how the jeep was kept in a state of repair without even an amateur mechanic within 40 miles.

Mother Eliza could visit the few villages along her "jeep road" like Pajebotown, but she probably realized before too long that it was not a practical venture. The climate and humidity is very hard on any kind of machinery in Liberia—added to the lack of mechanical training of the people. The maintenance of equipment is a nightmare of frustration even today.

Mother used the jeep for several years herself, and then turned it over to one of the boys who was attending high school in Sinoe. At some stage it ran backward down a hill and was damaged beyond the abilities of the local garage to repair. Eventually it was sold to another American missionary, who hopefully was able to make better use of it.

During this time Mother continued to carry a heavy load of teaching, gardening, and especially writing to keep her friends back in America in touch with the work. There was never a time when she could slack off from this, for that communication was the lifeline to her ministry.

Her sister Jenny Belle had agreed to be the channel for all funds sent to her, and Mother marveled at her careful accounting and faithful reporting. Once when she went home to Texas she saw a jar of Vaseline sitting on a shelf above her bed in her room, and she asked Jenny Belle why she hadn't used it. "Well, sister, it's yours, and you never told me to use it," was the frank reply.

But Mother knew that Jenny Belle worried about her in Africa at this old age, and so she kept a regular stream of cheerful and newsy letters going back to her.

Her friends in the government sometimes worried about her too, and wondered how long she could continue to serve in their midst. Perhaps with this thought in mind the Minister of the Interior, the now-Senator Harrison Grigsby, suggested to President Tubman that it would seem the time had come to decorate Mother Eliza George for her service to God and country.

A surprise program was planned in Greenville, which was to be in the superintendent's office. Though President Tubman could not come, Vice President Green (who was then governor of Sinoe County), Senator Harrison Grigsby, and many of the county officials were present. As Senator Grigsby described Mother Eliza's reactions to the whole affair, "Mother is a woman who is never excited about anything. She was calm and cool under almost any situation. But when she heard the citation read, she wept."

> For the many contributions you have made towards the people of Sinoe, particularly the unlettered people of the country, and because of the sacrifices you have undergone . . . I do confer upon Eliza Davis-George the grade of Knight office for the Redemption of Africa.

A bright red, green, and white ribbon, the badge of the order of knighthood, was then placed across her chest, looking somewhat incongruous against her simple print house dress. The Senator then pinned a large silver brooch on her shoulder which bore the motto of the Liberian Republic, THE LOVE OF LIBERTY BROUGHT US HERE.

As she stood before her children and before the high government officials and friends she had known for many years, bedecked in the nation's finery for one of the few times in her life, Mother was speechless.

But the crowning point of that year came when she watched the graduating class of the College of Liberia and heard her own Augustus delivering the valedictory speech. It had been a joy to be able to provide him a spotless white suit and black bow tie with matching boutonniere for the occasion. After the graduation Mother and Gus had formal portraits made to commemorate the event.

In California, Madie Monroe had been able to raise enough money for Gus's ticket, and this time, with his graduation diploma laden with honors to present to the consulate, there was no difficulty in obtaining a student's visa.

And so the "Eliza Davis George Club" of faithful black women in California provided the affidavit required and guaranteed Gus's support during his stay in the United States. They promised Mother that they would house and care for him and still continue to help Mother as best they could. Without their sacrificial help, Gus would never have gone overseas to study.

So Mother now "carried" yet another child back to the U.S.A., and her 74-year-old heart could not deny that she was pinning all her hopes on him.

chapter twenty four

Romance in San Francisco

Eliza hobbled into her room after the evening prayers in the dining room. Now that she had several good teachers to help the children, she did not have to stay to supervise the studies, as she used to. There were always so many letters to answer, and of late she was finding it hard to see well enough to write. The pages became blurry in front of her eyes. "I probably need a change of glasses," she thought. "I'll have to have a checkup next time I go to Greenville."

In years past she had to wait until she got back to the United States, but now there was an eye doctor connected with the government hospital in Greenville.

The next time Eliza got into Greenville she went to the simple government hospital on the outskirts of town and asked for the eye doctor. He might be able to send for new glasses from Monrovia, she thought.

But the doctor checked first one eye and then the other, taking far longer than any eye examination had ever taken before. Finally he sat on his high round stool and folded his hands in front of him. "I'm afraid, Mrs. George, you need an operation immediately—and it is one we are not equipped to do here in Liberia."

Eliza froze in her seat as the doctor went on. "You have advanced cataracts, and unless you have that operation within a few months, you will be totally blind."

In a daze, Eliza stumbled out of his office and back toward the main street of Greenville. He was asking the impossible. There had been very little money coming in lately, and with the large staff and almost 70 children on the mission, every cent was gone. Where would she find money for her fare home? Of course she could write and tell her friends about the need, but that would take three of four months at the earliest for a reply.

Could she borrow the money? Not from anyone here in Greenville—she had already stretched her credit as far as she could with the local shopkeepers. They trusted her, and they knew that she would eventually pay back every cent she borrowed, but she doubted that they would forward several hundred dollars for a boat trip to the United States.

But Eliza's lifelong habit of faith was still operable, and, shooting a prayer heavenward, she headed for the post office to pick up this week's mail.

The little post office near the river's edge was usually a bustle of cheerful talk and gathering of friends as they waited for the slow-moving clerks to sort the mail and put it into the dusty cubicles behind the counter. As Mother came up to the counter, she didn't engage in the usual banter with the young clerks she had known since they were runny-nosed children hanging around outside the shops on mainstreet.

"Son, is there any mail for Mother this morning?"

The clerk sauntered over to her box and came back empty-handed. "Nothing, Mother, but a new batch has just come in. Do you want me to look through that for you?"

"Yes, be a darling and go see. Mother needs some mail real bad this morning."

It was really no surprise to Eliza to open the envelope from a church in Texas and find a check for $600. And it was no surprise for the people in the post office to hear Mother shout "Praise the Lord!" as she hopped out the door and down the street.

When she arrived in Monrovia, there was still one more obstacle to overcome—she needed immediate passage on a ship to the United States. She came back to explain her plans to Ora, who seemed to be more worried about Mother's eye problem than she was.

"Dearie, the Lord has answered prayer again. The agent said the passenger ship was gone for this month, but there is a cargo ship in the harbor due to sail the day after tomorrow. He asked if I would be willing to take that. I just told him, 'I'll go on anything. I've got to get to the States because they tell me I'm going blind.'"

The operation, which was paid for by friends in the Morning Star Baptist Church in Chicago, was successful, and for months afterward Mother would show the little bottle containing her cataracts wherever she went.

Of course she had to see Gus while she was in the United States, and as soon as she could arrange her itinerary, she headed for San Francisco.

In Mother's usual independent way, she didn't tell me about her coming to the United States, or her serious cataract operation until it was all over. How I praised the Lord that He had spared her eyesight! The operation explained why her letters had been so difficult to read in recent months; I had been wondering if she had suddenly become afflicted with all the usual signs of old age that other people endure. It was a relief to know that it was a reversible symptom and that her sight had been spared.

But I must confess I anticipated Mother's visit with mixed emotions, for though I longed to see her and talk with her, I was not sure she would be happy about my news.

I was now in my first year at Golden Gate Seminary after completing a B.A. at Simpson College. The M.R.E. program would take me two years, and then I would be going back to Liberia. I could hardly wait.

But something unforeseen and unplanned had happened in my life—I was in love.

It all happened so naturally and innocently that neither one of us could say just when it started. Well, I guess you could say it started that morning when I was asked to speak in chapel and tell about my burden for Liberia. I know God spoke through me that morning, for there were many wet eyes in the congregation, and students came up to me for weeks afterward to comment on what they had heard.

But that morning a young lady waited around after chapel until I was free to talk with her to tell me how deeply touched she had been by my message and how she had been praying herself about going to Africa as a missionary. She wondered if there would be some time when I could tell her more about the requirements and conditions and perhaps pray with her about her decision.

We began to meet. The first time was just a general conversation, and we realized that there was much to talk and pray over, so we planned to meet twice a week in one of the upstairs classrooms. We read the Word of God together and began sharing experiences from our Christian life and how God had been leading us.

Before we knew it Donna and I were deeply involved with each other. I guess I really admitted it the first time she was absent from a class we had together, and I could think of nothing else but "where is she?"

From then on we seemed to spend more and more time together—in the dining hall, study hall. It was just a natural step to begin thinking of marriage and praying for God's guidance in this momentous step.

Realizing it posed some special problems for us, we wanted to seek counsel from someone outside the Southern Baptist leadership at the school, for we knew what their attitude toward mixed marriage would be. We wanted someone who would be totally objective—and I guess really wanted someone who would see the whole thing from our perspective.

Donna had a friend from her hometown of Portland, Oregon, whom she deeply respected, and one weekend we went to visit

Mrs. Schmidt. Listening carefully to our story, this dear lady of God wisely steered us on a neutral course. She said she could see no objection, but that we would have to pray more about it and be willing to face up to the possible problems an interracial marriage might cause. She pointed out that many people would not understand or approve and that we had to take that into consideration.

So we were back to the beginning. We knew we could go no further with our plans until we had told Mother Eliza. And now here she was, unexpectedly in the United States, and on her way to see me. I was afraid I knew what she was going to say, but somehow hoping against hope that when she met Donna, she would change her mind.

Of course Mother didn't change her mind. She had always been convinced that interracial marriages were not God's plan—hadn't He determined the bounds of their habitations (Acts 17:26)?

As she and Gus and Donna spoke together, her heart went out to the two young people, so obviously in love, and yet so desirous of pleasing and serving God. But Mother had always been firm with her children, and this was no exception.

"Children, this is not God's will that you marry each other. Gus has a call from God to return to his own people in the interior of Liberia to take God's message to them. He needs a wife who will understand those people, who knows their customs. You may think, Donna, that you can do those things, but you never will. Those Liberians have hardly ever seen a white woman—you will be strange to them, and they will never understand you. You will become homesick for your own people, and Gus will be caught between pleasing you and obeying God. No, children, Mother cannot give her permission for this marriage."

The young couple assured her they would consider her advice seriously and pray objectively about it, but they did not promise to break their relationship.

Mother returned to Liberia wondering if her friend's dire predictions about sending Gus to the U.S.A. would come true after all.

chapter twenty five

Mother Picks a Wife

When Mother returned to ENI this time, it was to the happy news that one of her "boys," Jeremia Lewis, who had been studying in Monrovia with Gus, had now returned to assist Charles Carpenter in the work. With some 60 children in the school and two motherless babies to care for, there never seemed to be enough help.

Mother wrote to one of her friends back in the U.S., "I am working on the road. It is a real task, but we mean to get through it some way. We walked one night last week accompanied by two of our boys from 4 a.m. to 4 p.m., and how tired we were at the end of our journey! We hope to get the road fixed so that we can drive the jeep and not have to walk so far."

The jeep had been immobilized for some time, but though Mother never again drove it, there was that constant hope that one day she would be on wheels again.

The joy of seeing new converts in the villages come to Christ offset the sorrow of losing two babies within that year of 1959—both had been brought in the villagers after the mother died in childbirth. Tribal belief held that the dead mother became a witch whose spirit traveled around in the night, and the villagers wanted nothing to do with the baby which might attract her spirit.

It was probably in these traumatic experiences of seeing a helpless infant dying in her arms, with no medical care available, that Mother's dream of a maternity clinic first originated. But that was far from the realm of possibility, for now her own house was ready to fall around her ears. She had never had a substantial home in Africa in the 47 years she had lived there, but the California club was now raising money for such a project. Cement blocks were actually being made.

With all the activity and problems of running the mission, Mother's heart continued to ache about Gus's future. She knew it was a difficult decision to make, and when his letter finally arrived, she really couldn't predict what his decision would be.

After Mother left, Donna and I continued to meet, but our talk of marriage and the future had a hollow ring to it. Both of us respected Mother too much to discount what she had said. I think from the beginning we realized that Mother was right. God had a special task for me to do in Africa, and I would be sidetracked with a white American wife who might find life in the African jungle very strange and might eventually want to return home.

When we finally decided to break off the relationship, Donna transferred to another college. We both felt the situation to be too emotionally taxing, and since I was aiming at graduation in May of 1960, it was not possible for me to transfer to another school without losing credits.

But even while Donna was away she wrote me several very touching letters. She still felt that we could have served the Lord together in Africa.

When Mother returned to the U.S. for Gus's graduation—a trip that had been planned long before the emergency trip for her cataract operation—she carried in her purse pictures of two of her "daughters" on the mission. Eliza had prayed much about a wife for Gus, for she realized that his ministry would be limited unless he were married. Tribal people do not consider a man fully mature until he has a wife and child, and Gus would need all the credibility he could muster for the task ahead of him.

The graduation was an exciting time, filled with a deep sense of pride as Mother was told over and over what a wonderful contribution her son had made on the campus. Their picture appeared in the School paper together, and an article was written about Gus in *Christian Life* magazine. Mother met many students who had been part of a weekly prayer meeting for Liberia, and it touched her heart to think that these white young folks cared enough about her people in Africa to pray specifically for ENI's needs.

When the excitement had finally died down, and Mother and Gus were alone, she brought up the subject of a wife for him.

"You know, Gustus, that you will need to marry if you are to have the respect of the men in the villages. Also, many of the girls on the mission are young misses now, and it might be a temptation to them if you were unmarried.

"So, I'm suggesting that you choose one of these two girls. I've thought and prayed over this a lot, and I think either one of them would make you a good wife. They are both fine, dedicated Christian girls; they have been with me for quite a few years, and I have trained them to be good housewives and taught them all I know."

She placed two pictures before him on the table. He knew both of them, but neither really well. They were both attractive Liberian country girls, and he was sure that Mother had made her choice carefully and with much prayer.

Picking up the pictures, he thanked Mother for her care for him, and said he would have to think and pray about it.

I really didn't need very long to think about it, for though I didn't know Otheliah well, I had always admired her sister, Annie. She was married to Otto Klebo. Annie had been the gentlest, meekest girl I'd known, with just the qualities I'd always wanted in a wife. If Otheliah was anything like her sister, she would be just right for me.

And she was beautiful too, with that heart-shaped face and large round eyes that gleamed with a hint of mischief even in the poor picture Mother brought.

I told Mother that Otheliah was my choice and asked her to write to her for me.

Otheliah confesses that she was quite taken by surprise when Mother's letter reached her at Seuhn Academy, where Mother had sent her for her high-school training. She says, "I knew Gus and used to call him Brother Gus when he taught us in Sunday school. He had never shown one bit of interest in me when he had come to ENI to visit.

"Mother told me to let her know whether I would marry Gus, but I didn't know what to say. Before I could answer I got another letter telling me that she was anxiously awaiting my reply. I decided to tell her that if Gus wants to marry me, let him write me himself."

I wasn't surprised at Otheliah's answer. I remembered her with just that kind of spunk, and I was glad for that. After my years in

America I would find it hard to get used to a girl who just agreed to everything I said, with never an idea of her own. So I sat down to compose one of the most important letters of my life. Even to this day I can just about remember it word for word:

> Dear Otheliah,
>
> Having discussed with Mother Eliza about the work and about the girl I should marry, Mother talked so highly about you that I decided to get married to you.
>
> I've known you on the mission and I've been impressed with the life of your sister. So when Mother shared with me about the kind of girl you are, I fell deeply in love with you, and I would like to get married to you.
>
> By the grace of God I plan to come home this year, and I would like to get married right away. May God bless you.
>
> Yours truly,
> Augustus

When I left Monrovia in November, 1960, I carried in my pocket a well-worn letter of acceptance from the girl who had agreed to be my wife, and a beautiful picture which I showed to everyone who would look at it.

When I arrived in Monrovia, Otheliah was waiting for me at the Hortons, looking shy and a bit ill-at-ease, but even more beautiful than her picture.

chapter twenty six

Son, Take It

"How many times have letters brought news that shattered my life?" thought Eliza as she slowly put Gus's letter down on the table in front of her. It was January, 1961, and she was home with Jenny Belle in the little clapboard house that had belonged to her family all these years.

When Gus's letter arrived this morning, she had eagerly torn it open, for she hadn't heard from him since he had returned to Liberia. Was he happy with her choice of Otheliah for him? What were their wedding plans? How soon would he be going out to ENI?

She had read with pride the article about him in the *Christian Life* magazine. Granted, it had sounded a bit presumptuous: "After six years in the U.S. for education, Marwieh this month becomes director of the Elizabeth Native Interior Mission in Liberia."

Perhaps that was a bit premature, for Eliza intended to retain her leadership for a few years yet—at least until Augustus had been well-indoctrinated and properly introduced.

But now it seemed that once again her dreams were shattered. And she couldn't blame Gus; he had been placed in a difficult position. She read the paragraph from his letter once again:

Dr. Tolbert asked me to come and see him as soon as I arrived in Monrovia to discuss our relationship with the Southern Baptists. He took me in his limousine to visit Ricks Institute, the Liberian Baptist school on the outskirts of Monrovia. You know it, don't you, Mother? On the way there he asked me to teach at Ricks, since they are desperate for qualified staff. I was really taken aback, for you know how we planned for me to return to ENI. I told him I would need two weeks to think about it. What should I do, Mother?

Eliza could well understand Gus's predicament. Not only was Dr. William Tolbert the Vice President of Liberia, but he was the President of the Liberian Baptist Convention, and Ricks was a convention school, Naturally he would want a man of Gus' qualifications to teach at this important institution. How naive of her to think that she could keep this gifted and highly educated young man for her own little work out in the bush!

Instinctively she began praying aloud. Jenny Belle was used to hearing her sister's open conversations with her heavenly Father.

Dear Lord, You're the one who brought Gustus out of the interior to study at my mission. And now I need him to take over for me, Lord; I'm 82 years old, and the burden is getting too heavy for me to carry. But dear Jesus, if You need Gustus at Ricks more, then I know You can take care of ENI too. Bless Gustus today; guide and direct and protect the entire mission. Provide for Gustus as he takes on this great responsibility. May the angels who encamp about those who love and fear You encamp around him. Amen.

Gus had written Eliza a number of times during the previous two years about his desire to have the Southern Baptist Convention send missionaries to Liberia. While earning his M.R.E. at Golden Gate Seminary he had become familiar with their leadership and their mission program, and he believed that God could use them to alleviate the great spiritual and material needs in Liberia.

At first the leaders of the Baptist mission board refused; there were already three other Baptist groups working in Liberia, and furthermore they were planning to enter new fields in Angola and Mozambique.

But Gus would not take no for an answer. He had written and told Mother about the prayer groups he had organized, which met almost daily on campus to ask God to change the minds of the convention leaders. He had encouraged Mother to add her voice to Gus's pleas by writing Dr. Gearner, secretary for Africa of the Southern Baptist Mission Board. So she had written.

I have with and without support tried to keep alive the spark of missionary work until Augustus returned. Now the sun of my life is sinking on the going-down side, and I humbly appeal to you and your foreign mission board of the Southern Baptist Convention to share with the humble missionary endeavor in Sinoe County, Liberia, where Augustus is going, and strengthen it before it dies.

Suddenly miracles began happening: the governments of Angola and Mozambique refused the Southern Baptist's application to enter their countries; Dr. William Tolbert, Vice President of Liberia, heard about Gus's request and added his own appeal for help; finally, the leaders of the Southern Baptist Mission Board found themselves on the same plane with Dr. Tolbert when they flew to the Baptist World Alliance in Brazil. Certainly this was not just coincidence; all began to feel God's guidance.

So it was that when Gus returned to Liberia, arrangements had been made for the Southern Baptists to send missionaries to work with the Liberian Baptist Convention, and Gus was sure that ENI would benefit from this new relationship.

He had never dreamed that it would involve his own commitment. And his first response was to say no. He had been preparing to return to his own people in the bush for six years. All the time in America he had prayed fervently that he might not die like Sammy Morris, that great black missionary who died before he could ever return to Liberia.

Eliza knew what she must do. Even though Gus had asked the advice of missionaries in Monrovia (they had all urged him to accept the appointment), she knew he would not make a decision until he heard from her. Reaching for her handbag and cane, she pulled herself wearily to her feet.

"Jenny Belle," she called to her sister in the kitchen, "I'm going over to the post office. I won't be gone long."

The telegram she drafted was economically to the point: SON, TAKE IT.

She had one more task to complete on this January 28, 1961. Now that she had heard from Gustus, she must answer the letter of his friend, Mr. Finley.

Gus had written several months earlier: "Allen Finley, whom I met several years ago through International Students, has been taking me to churches where I could tell about the work at ENI. In fact, he has offered to arrange a deputation tour to help me raise funds for my passage back to Liberia."

The previous December, Eliza had received a letter from Allen Finley:

Dear Mother Eliza:

I am writing to you because of our mutual interest in our dear brother Augustus Marwieh. I am the general director of Christian Nationals' Evangelism Commission, the organization that helped him on his trip cross-country. The Lord richly blessed him and gave him some funds to help get him on his way back to Liberia, and we hope this will also mean some future support.

CNEC has helped native workers for twenty years. We have a wonderful board of godly men from across the nation who have sought to do this type of work, and the Lord has blessed it. We are now supporting about 105 native evangelists in Malaysia, Thailand, Singapore, and Hong Kong . . . and now we are also seeking to help Gus . . . . We are set up so that we do not maintain control over these men, but we seek to share with them in the work God has given them to do . . .

We are already set up in relation to Augustus, with funds going to him and toward the support of his work . . . . CNEC needs to release its funds to a mission, and certainly our desire is to release all we can raise for Brother Augustus to the ENI mission, but I would appreciate it if you would explain or send us some information on how this mission is set up . . . .

Eliza didn't know just what this new organization would be willing to do for ENI now that Gustus wouldn't be working there, but she owed Mr. Finley some kind of answer. She decided not to write about this latest development just yet.

Dear Mr. Finley,

Long ago you wrote me . . . . I was waiting to hear from Augustus . . . . I received a letter from him this week stating that he will marry on the 29th of this month. That is tomorrow. We pray God's blessing upon him and his choice for a companion in life. The Lord blessed me to humbly share a part in training both of them.

Now with regards to our work. It has been one of the struggles by faith in God that has helped us through his friends. I appreciate your interest in Augustus especially now, for this is the beginning of his new field of many difficulties.

Sixteen years ago the Liberian government gave me 500 acres of land for missionary purposes, and we have not done very much cultivating of the land so as to make the work self-supporting along the lines of agriculture. We do not have substantial buildings, but have erected country houses, have taught school on the main mission and out-stations, and have sent out native missionary workers.

It may be of interest to write that the 20th of this month was my 82nd birthday.

The next day, 100 miles away in Monrovia, the Hortons stood in for Mother and gave Otheliah and Gus a beautiful wedding in the St. Simon Baptist Church, where Mother had worshiped so many times over the years. Dr. Horton performed the ceremony, and the reception was held at their home, up the street from the church.

We had a Western wedding and then took a Western honeymoon—something unheard-of in the bush. A cottage was made available on the premises of ELWA, the Sudan Interior Mission radio station, whose beautiful campus stretches for almost a mile along the palm-lined beaches of the Atlantic Ocean.

I can say with a pure conscience before God that I never knew any other woman. I did not know Otheliah until our honeymoon. This was a "pure fact"—even though I did not get married until I was 33 years old. But God miraculously kept me. I spent time on my knees struggling; only God's miracle kept me. There were times when I was absolutely as weak as water, but by God's grace I was able. I could have fallen so many times.

chapter twenty seven

The Tribal Reunion

"Young man, I'll have you know I've been in this country longer than you are old. God sent me here, and if He sent me here, nothing can stop me." Seeing the startled look on the face of the young Liberian customs officer, Mother gave him a warm smile, adding, "Now you be a dear and just do what you have to."

Later, at the Hortons, Mother related the incident to Ora as the two old friends sat up late in the night catching up on all the news. "I guess I should have gotten a visa back in the States, but once I had enough for my flight, the only thing I oculd think of was to get back here." Then with a hearty chuckle she added, "But you know, dearie, they gave me my visa anyway. I just charmed them! . . . . Now tell me all about Gus's wedding."

On the surface Mother had not changed much. Her gray hair was pulled smoothly back from her face, her skin remarkably unwrinkled for her 82 years, though her cheeks had hollowed out to accentuate her determined chin. She still held herself erect, even though she had to resort to hopping when she wanted to move quickly, for her ulcerated leg continued to give her trouble.

She still gave the impression that she was very much in charge of any situation, but closer scrutiny would reveal an underlying weariness. Gus's appointment to Ricks had hit her harder than she had anticipated. She had fully expected to return to find him at ENI, carrying the heavy burden of the work, relieving her of the many decisions and daily cares of her growing mission family. She confessed to feeling in spirit like the song composed by the slaves: "Keep inching along like the poor inchworm; we'll get home by and by."

Besides the normal care of the school and churches, more and more motherless babies were being brought to her; several died on the mission during that year of 1961.

In a letter to one of her friends in the U.S. she said, "When I wrote you last our motherless mission baby was seriously ill. She now sleeps in the arms of Jesus. It is not an easy task to rear babies in this country, but we tried our best for this little one."

And when she announced the joyful news of the arrival of Gus and Otheliah's little son in the hospital in Monrovia, she added, "Where we are, the children share their part in sightseeing when a woman gives birth in their village."

In spite of her weariness, she began planning a mother's clinic, to be built on the station, where mothers and babies could be cared for.

Though Mother didn't fully comprehend the implications, she began receiving assistance from two organizations during that year which would eventually be the means of growth and expansion far beyond her fondest dreams.

Shortly after arriving back in Liberia she received the first regular monthly gift of $50 from Christian Nationals Evangelism Commission. The money had been given for Gus and his work, but since he was receiving a salary from Ricks, he had asked that it be sent to Mother Eliza at ENI.

In response to the first gift, Mother wrote to Allen Finley:

> Thanks much for your abiding interest. The gift sent by your board goes a long way to help . . . . Struggling for many years by faith with only God through a few friends here and there, you can imagine how much your assistance is appreciated.
>
> Thanks for your prayers. Saving souls and bringing up the moral side and character-building can by no means be considered an easy task. Gus and I have always been one in the Lord along this line.
>
> Just one week ago Josiah, our assistant teacher to Charles on the mission, triumphantly passed to the other side. Noiselessly he did his living best in everything he was called upon to do. We miss him.
>
> We have 85 day students. Before going to the U.S. we had 65 boarders, but the responsibility is too great now.
>
> One week ago the Lord blessed us with six lovely converts. They went with Him in baptism.
>
> Chiefs in the interior are begging us to send missionaries to teach their children. So many children have never seen a schoolroom, and many grown-ups further on have not yet heard the sweet story of Jesus and his never-dying love. Pray much for us . . . our cares are many.
>
> Four of our boys are attending school at the beach; they are writing me of their needs. Thirteen churches

(each with a national worker) plus 25 boarding children, 85 day pupils, and one motherless baby present the need for Bibles, songbooks, and schoolbooks. There is also a $300 debt. Jesus says, "Owe no man."

It may be of interest to write that a white couple will soon come to Sinoe to help us. Praise the Lord for His goodness. This couple we believe too has the Christlike spirit.

It is now after 1 a.m. At early morn after prayer three of us are to begin our tramp to Greenville.

> Yours trusting,
> Mother Eliza George

Shortly after this, Mother visited one of her newly established national churches, using the same old "ankle express" that had served her for so many years. It was an eight-hour walk through swollen rivers, over foot logs and a pouring rain. But she still felt the urgent need to keep in touch with her "missionary children" and to encourage them in their work. At this church she was faced with yet another request for a school; more than a hundred church children had no such opportunity. The burden was almost more than she could bear, but she must find a way to start another school.

Back in Monrovia, Gus and Otheliah had settled into the fine house provided by the Institute; Gus even had a car. He was happy to be able to provide his lovely young wife with the comforts of the city—electricity, shopping convenience, running water—all the things she would never have had out at ENI.

But he was deeply disturbed at the thought of Mother struggling alone out there on the mission while he worked comfortably in the city. Rev. Poe, who was the first Southern Baptist missionary to be sent to Liberia under the arrangements made after Gus's request, was the principal of Ricks. Noting that Gus was uncomfortable about the turn of events, Poe urged the Southern Baptists to send someone to help Mother Eliza "or we will lose him."

Thus it was that by September of 1961, John and Betty Carpenter arrived to help Mother Eliza with the church work. John and Gus flew to Greenville together and from there drove to Plahn to meet with Mother and the church leaders. Gus captured the excitement of his first visit home when he wrote:

> (portions of letters)
>
> My dear Friends,
>
> A very moving, dramatic scene was made on the 21st of October when I visited my tribal people for

the first time since my return from the U.S. People from all over the surrounding and distant villages traveled miles to come to see me and Rev. Carpenter, an American missionary whom God has sent to help us carry on the labor of love among my people. The sight was one of the rarest I have ever seen. The people display all kinds of emotions, each according to his peculiar emotional constitution. Some sang, some danced, while others cried profusely. Sometimes they hugged me, sometimes they picked me up, and sometimes some tried to carry me on their backs. When I saw so many people, most of whom have no relationship to me except by tribe, going so wild about me, I was overpowered by the thought of how my father, my mother, my brother, or my uncle would have felt if they were living.

The time of reunion with my people was one of the happiest moments in my life. It was incredible to think that I, who less than nineteen years ago left home as a boy, almost completely naked, could return to my people with a Master's Degree, shoes on my feet, a tie on my neck, and dressed in a suit. I left home believing in superstitions and witchcrafts and returned as an ordained minister with a gospel message. Can you imagine that?

When the Carpenters moved out to Greenville later that year, they were to be the first white missionaries to work with Mother Eliza. Carpenter had come primarily to assist with the development of the church work, and to relieve Mother of that responsibility.

But she soon encouraged him to handle her funds as well; he became, in a sense, her business manager.

She jokingly referred to him as "the great white elephant," and for the first time in her ministry could send people to someone else when they came asking for help.

Carpenter admits that Mother was good-hearted. "She just didn't realize that people were taking advantage of her . . . . I put her on a budget and made available only a certain amount of money to be spent on materials, etc. When her helpers came down to get supplies, for the first time in her years in Africa she was able to operate in the black, and that was simply because I defended her from those who would take advantage of her."

But Carpenter was quick to praise Mother Eliza for her overwhelming love for people. "No one could ever question Mother Eliza's love. And that love caused her to go to any extent to try to provide an education opportunity for them.

> "Interestingly, before we got to Liberia I had a vision of her being very brittle, cantankerous, overbearing, and demanding, and I had a fear of having difficulty in working with her. When we got there, we found her just the opposite.
>
> "One thing stands out . . . she was so jovial, so deeply spiritual. She could go through the longest periods of fasting and praying . . . she had a sense of humor about everything . . . ."

By and large Carpenter felt that the African church leaders whom Mother had raised were good men but had little training. "I never had any quarrel with Mother on her theology or Biblical interpretation," he explained. "She approached the Scriptures from a devotional standpoint. She bathed herself in the Scriptures."

But the men needed more systematic training in the Word of God, and this Carpenter began to do.

Now instead of Gus feeling sorry for Mother, Mother began feeling sorry for Gus. During the first year back at ENI, Mother had sent eight mission children to stay with the Marwiehs in Monrovia; one was a mission baby whose uncle had threatened to steal and sell her. Gus was struggling, so Mother wrote to CNEC:

> I wonder if Gus has more on his toes than he can kick off his heels. He is now acting principal as well as teaching at Ricks. He has eleven mouths to feed, including his wife and children. I took $13.50 of the $50 sent by CNEC and sent Dessie to Gus. I should be sending something to help Gus but do not have it. He, like myself, accepts more upon him than he is able to do. I still believe the $50 should go to help Gus and his wife.

In August, Mother spent some time in the Greenville hospital. The ulcer on her leg had been irritated by a cat's scratch, and the infection had eaten right down to the bone. For the rest of her life it continued to trouble her; several times doctors threatened to amputate the foot, but Mother wouldn't hear of it. There was still no road the last 12 miles through the jungle to ENI, and she was determined to keep walking as long as God gave her strength.

When Gus came to help John Carpenter with a pastor's Bible school at ENI, his heart was encouraged to see what a load had been lifted from Mother's shoulders. There were not 16 pastors, and even though there were no substantial buildings, the churches were growing.

Gus also brought some exciting news for Mother—at least he thought it was exciting.

"The Southern Baptists have decided to make a 30-minute television program about your work at ENI, Mother. They want you to come back to Monrovia with us to film it there, since they can't get their equipment out here to ENI."

But Mother was aghast. "No, son, I don't think I should do that. The Lord has given us this work, and He doesn't want us to take any glory for it. That would be wrong for me to put myself forward like that."

But Gus and Carpenter wouldn't rest until they had convinced Mother that the TV program would not be glorifying her, but would promote her beloved work. When she finally acquiesced, she became as excited as they were about the prospects. The TV crew loved her for her natural acting ability and for her boundless wit. Narrated in the United States after the filming was complete, Mother was not aware how prestigious a commentator would introduce her to the American public.

> Hello, Americans—I'm Paul Harvey . . . my newscast is over for today, but I have another story . . . the struggle to conquer the American frontier . . . . That struggle was repeated on a new frontier—Liberia—by other Americans, by negroes like Mother Eliza George . . . .
>
> As the Liberian nation looks to a sure and prosperous future, Mother Eliza George looks at the two men, Augustus and John . . . and knows that the work she began 50 years ago will continue to grow.

By the time the program was televised in the Southern Baptists' series, "The Answer," in March of 1963, Mother had returned to the U.S. with yet another baby. Struggling with wet diapers, bottles, and a fussy baby, she took a third motherless child on the long journey to the States to be placed in a Christian home to be educated there. She had hidden hope that perhaps one of them would return to their own people to one day serve God and help their people, but none of them ever did.

Once again Mother Eliza was back on the deputation trail. She left Keturah with a family in Illinois who adopted her and then began in earnest representing the needs at ENI. Her goal before the end of the year was to raise enough money to erect three substantial buildings on the campus—one for the boys, a chapel, and a building for motherless babies.

Gus had asked his friend, Allen Finley, to help Mother make arrangements for meetings, but it would be August before CNEC was able to catch up with Mother's busy schedule. In a quick note explaining what she had been doing, she wrote:

"I had my last meeting in Chicago on the 21st of August. Then I ran down to Toccoa and Maritta, Georgia, on the 23rd and returned to Chicago on the 27th."

Not only was CNEC trying to contact her, but Sherwood Wirt was eager to interview her for an article for *Decision* magazine. Mother traveled to the Minneapolis headquarters of the Billy Graham Association and spent several hours with editor Wirt, and her story appeared in the February, 1964, issue of *Decision*. The article closed with her impassioned appeal for help:

> We need nurses over there. We need medical missionaries. We need houses for motherless babies. I am in Chicago right now seeking funds, but I yearn to get back to Africa so badly. It is a great country, and it needs Christ. The Africans see what we are doing, and they look up at the moon and sun and stars and say, "Big man up yonder." But they don't know Him! So many have a zeal, but not according to knowledge. Pray for them! And pray that God will raise up more young American Negro Christians to minister to their brethren in the land of their fathers.

After years of deputation in American black churches, she had come to the conclusion, "Our people on this side have such a limited vision of the work to be done over there."

So she threw herself even more enthusiastically into meetings, speaking in every black church that would give her opportunity. She had planned to return to Africa early in 1964, but then tragedy struck.

Sister Ellen, who had been living with Jenny Belle for many years, suddenly became ill, and in a few days was gone. Sorrowful, Eliza returned to Taylor to share in the family's grief, little realizing that Ellen's death would mark the end of her permanent ministry in Africa. Though she would return to Africa a number of times in the next nine years, she would remain the head of ENI in name only.

Eliza truly believed that this is what she wanted—she had prayed for a replacement for years—but she was nevertheless very hurt when she realized that her leadership was no longer needed.

chapter twenty eight

Back to the Jungle

I felt so sorry for Mother. After Ellen died she stayed another six months with Jenny Belle, trying to help her adjust to the great loss. Jenny had always been close to Mother; in fact, had faithfully forwarded funds and channeled receipts to Mother's donors for many years. Mother could not have carried on without her, especially after the National Baptists retired her.

So now, of course, she felt responsible for taking care of Jenny Belle. They were the only two of the 11 Davis children still living.

Cecelia was living in Austin, just 30 minutes' drive away, and she did what she could to keep an eye on Jenny. But Cecelia had three children and was holding down a job, so it wasn't easy to run back and forth frequently.

By May, Mother felt Jenny was strong enough to be left alone, and so she returned to Africa. I think she felt she was losing her grip on the work and needed to get back.

But she had only been in Africa a month when she received an urgent message to return to Texas: Jenny Belle had had a serious nervous breakdown. And so far the third time in one month my 87-year-old spiritual mother flew halfway around the world.

Though Charles Carpenter was doing a fine job of carrying on the school at ENI, I was becoming more and more exercised about the spiritual darkness among the tribal people in the interior of Liberia. The coastal areas had been evangelized for many years; yet I could still remember how my mother, Nyonabe, had invited strangers from Grand Gedeh to stop and rest while she prepared a meal for them. As a boy I would hang around listening to the men tell their tales of war; I was intrigued by their strong-sounding dialect and different ways.

Yet, as far as I knew, no one had gone back to those people with the gospel; they were dying in darkness while I had been so richly blessed in Christ.

Though these thoughts kept nagging at me, it wasn't until a night in January, 1965, that the issue came to a head. I couldn't sleep, but lay tossing and turning far into the night. Even with the electric fan clattering in the open window, the air was thick and muggy—a typical Liberian night, and I had known many of them.

A picture of an old man kept passing across my mind—the old man I had met on the trail as I walked back to ENI last time. The trails were overgrown, barely visible in the thick jungle bush. It was a long, arduous walk to the clearing, where a dozen thatched huts were clustered.

The old man had been lying outside the door of his hut at the edge of the village, a ragged, mud-colored blanket covering his skeletal frame. When he opened his eyes, as I approached, they were like two luminous holes sunk deep into his head. I had not intended to stop here; I had hoped to meet the chief and his counselors and arrange a gathering of the whole village as soon as the people came in from their fields.

But something compelled me to stop and kneel beside the obviously suffering figure. "Old father," I said gently, putting my hand on the frail shoulder, "I've come to tell you of the great Father above who loves you."

The luminous eyes burned into mine as I shared Christ and His healing touch, inwardly wondering if my words were penetrating. When I finished praying, the old man called out, "Woman, come here."

An equally frail-looking woman appeared in the doorway of the hut. "Get the box!"

Without a word she disappeared into the hut and returned with a battered tin chest. Almost reverently the old man opened the lid and began taking out strange and exotic articles: a polished stone, a greasy woven pouch from which a pungent odor emanated, some gaudy beads, and a grotesque wooden image.

Taken aback, I recognized the tools of trade of a powerful witch doctor, and I wondered whether the old man was going to use them to try to drive me and my message of God away.

But the old man, handling the artifacts one by one, replacing them in the box almost lovingly, suddenly turned the chest upside down on the ground and commanded, "Woman, burn them. The God of heaven this man has told me about doesn't need my magic."

Over and over, the transformed face of the old man came to my mind as I lay on my sweat-stained bed, and I knew what God was saying: "Gus, it's time to go back to your people in the jungle. You've had that vision for many years, and now is my time. There are thousands like that old man who need to hear of me, and you are the one to go and tell them."

I knew the day had come, but did I still want to go? I looked over at Otheliah, asleep at my side. She deserved the nice home here at the Institute, with electricity and servants. And ruefully I had to admit that the chauffeur-driven car was a luxury I would miss. In the jungle one walked!

As I lay there I rationalized: these city young people were the future leaders of Liberia. It was important that they have dedicated Christian teachers. There were few enough of those in Liberia.

*Perhaps I was just being sentimental. People with lesser education and gifts could certainly work among those primitive village people who still lived on the same subsistence level they had a hundred years ago. Perhaps I could raise money to hire pastors (but there are no pastors out there); perhaps I could send literature out to the villages (but they can't read); or perhaps I could find someone else with the vision for those tribal people (but I've given **you** the vision, Gus).*

Would Otheliah agree to go back?

The first thing in the morning I told her of my long struggle and decision and I asked her, "Will you return to ENI with me, Otheliah? It won't be easy—you know how isolated and backward it is."

But Mother Eliza had chosen my wife well; she knew the caliber of the woman God had given me. Otheliah answered without a moment's hesitation, "If God is leading us to go, let's go."

There was still one more obstacle: Dr. William Tolbert, then vice president, had asked me to join the staff, and I felt I should receive his permission to resign. That very morning I excused myself from my classes and went to his office. He had often told me to come see him at any time; even though he was an extremely busy man, he wanted me to feel free to call upon him. That morning he was just on his way out to inspect a government project, and he invited me along. Riding in the back of his limousine, the window between us and the drive pulled shut for privacy, I poured out my heart to him.

I don't think he had ever really heard the story of my background, and what I owed to Mother Eliza. But when I finished telling him about my decision, he answered as a true Christian, "If God is leading you, then who am I to stand between you and the Lord?"

I was jubilant and began putting things in motion to speed my release. There was just one little matter I hadn't quite figured out—who would support me and my family?

The obvious answer to me was the Southern Baptists; they had come to Liberia at my instigation; I was working at Ricks, which had become their special project; one of their missionaries was in charge of Mother's churches. It seemed so logical.

But when I broached the subject, I was jolted to reality. South Baptist policy did not allow the mission to support a national worker; that was the responsibility of the churches. I was told to think it through very carefully. "You have a family . . . those children of yours have a future. Where will you get support if you leave Ricks? The Bible tells us to count the cost before we make a move. Don't jeopardize your family for a foolish dream."

But my mind was made up; with or without their support I would return to ENI. I made arrangements to leave Ricks in September. I knew that God had taken care of Mother Eliza all these years, and I could certainly trust Him to take care of me.

Just before leaving Monrovia, the thought came to me that I ought to write Allen Finley at CNEC; perhaps they would consider helping me expand the work at ENI. Before there was time for a response for him, Otheliah and I were back at ENI.

What a welcome! The jubilation of my first return with Carpenter was nothing compared to the love poured out to me and my family when my tribe learned that I had come home to stay. From surrounding villages miles away groups came in day after day bringing gifts of rice, chickens, goats, cassavas. We received so many chickens that we had to build a special house to keep them. For a month the celebrations continued, and we had enough food to keep our family for the rest of the year. That was God's first answer to our prayer for provision for my family.

Then came a letter from Allen Finley saying that he and two of his board members would be coming out to Liberia to visit ENI, and that if they were satisfied with what they saw, they would consider assisting the work to meet our current needs.

But there were problems too. My dear friend John Carpenter and I had to come to the parting of the ways. It was a friendly parting, for we loved each other in the Lord. But he wasn't happy about my working independent of the Southern Baptists at ENI, and I think he was a little concerned that I expected to take over the leadership of Mother's churches as well.

I didn't want that; John was doing a fine job training the pastors, and there were now 27 churches in the Eliza George Baptist Association. So we agreed that the churches would stay with the Liberian Baptists (with whom the Southern Baptists were working) and that I would take charge of the ENI mission. Of course, I planned to plant new churches, but wasn't there the whole unreached interior to work in?

Just about that time Mother came back to Liberia for a visit. She could only stay a few months because she did not dare leave Jenny for long. She still carried on a busy deputation schedule, raising her own travel funds as well as funds for the mission.

For the first time I sensed a little strain between Mother and me. I didn't realize it until several years later, but she feared two giants were taking over her work, and that I was contributing to their takeover.

ENI had so long been Mother's full responsibility; she had given her life to see it grow, had suffered physical pain and hunger, had wept copious tears in prayer, had fasted days on end—all to bring salvation and education to the "native children," as she so enduringly called them.

Now her age limited her leadership, and my return to ENI (the very thing she had been praying about for years) was taking her beloved work out of her control. Though her mind was alert, it seemed that she was more easily influenced by people around her.

Nevertheless, we had some good times while she was there, and she was able to meet Mr. Brewer, one of the CNEC board members, who had stayed longer than Mr. Finley and Elton Fox, another CNEC board member. When Mr. Brewer left, she was convinced (at least for the time being) of the wisdom of working with CNEC.

While Mr. Finley was here a wonderful thing happened. Delegates of the Shaw tribe came with a letter signed by the paramount chiefs, clan chiefs, and elders of Seekon and Tafjuezen chiefdoms, stating:

> Whereas the ENI Mission is dedicated to the spread of the gospel of the Lord Jesus Christ and to the education and training of our children and to the development of the resources of the land for the benefit of our people and to the bringing of medical help to our districts, we do hereby attest that we have given to the ENI mission for their permanent use and development 8000 acres of land, beginning from Samunien of Plandabale bo Town and Pebleh Town, Nyarn, to the southeast.

The letter was signed with the crosses and signatures of 16 village elders. Visions of cocoa and coffee plantations, enabling ENI to become self-sufficient, danced in my head. And when CNEC wrote some months later to say they had agreed to send $350 a month to support the running costs of ENI, I was confident that Mother's work was finally on a solid financial foundation.

Before many months had passed, I took a 150-mile hike into the interior, carrying the light of the gospel to those unreached people. They responded with such a movement of God that we saw 30 churches established and leaders appointed in each one. Mother's dreams for evangelizing Liberia were at last coming true.

chapter twenty nine

Lights to Share

Eliza had never liked traveling by hammock; it gave her such a helpless feeling swinging in the air, suspended between four men picking their way along the jungle trail.

"Why, what if they trip over a stump or step on a snake?" she used to argue with her husband. "They'd spill me right out on the ground."

If the truth were told, Eliza was just too independent to place herself so totally into someone else's hands. But this morning as the file of porters wound slowly through the jungle, Mother was glad she had given in. She would be 90 in just a few months, and though she could still walk many miles, this trip to Gbaizon might have been a little more than her old body could take.

Mother's body was old, but she did not believe in pampering herself. It had been tempered to finest steel as she pushed it to the limits of its endurance. Her friends used to marvel at the kind of chemistry God used to put her together.

It was just because of this marvelous resilience and strength that Gus had felt free to ask her along on this arduous journey into Gbaizon.

The tribe had sent a representation to the mission when Gus returned to ENI almost three years ago, begging him to visit their area. As soon as he had been able to free himself from the responsibilities at ENI, he and a group of pastors had taken the 150-mile hike through the Gbaizon area, where people had never heard the gospel.

When Gus told her the story, Mother had wept. How well she remembered her first visits to the villages around Kelton: her warm welcome, the eagerness with which the villagers heard her story, and the shame when they asked her outright, "Mammy, how long you people know about this Jesus?"

The Krohns in the Gbaizon area had responded to the gospel with such wholehearted abandon that 30 congregations had been formed during Gus's monthlong trip.

And now the women of the tribe had sent a message to ENI: "Come and bring some women to preach to us; you have sent men but never a woman. We want to learn more about God's Word too and how to change our ways."

It did not seem at all strange to Eliza that the Krohn women wanted to hear from a woman. After all, their lives were so different from their husbands; and there was so little real communication between the sexes in tribal life. Each had their distinct role to play; how could a man understand the tensions of two or three wives living together? The jealousies? The fears? Being accused of witchcraft or being cursed in pregnancy?

Being a woman had never limited Eliza's ambitions or dreams for her ministry; she had never questioned that God intended for her to use every ability, strength, and opportunity He had given her.

She gave deference to ministers; she was glad to have them preach and baptize whenever she could. But most of the time there simply were no men to preach or teach, to counsel or advise, to discipline, or even to farm and build in the places that God had called Eliza.

Somehow in spite of her strength and domineering tendencies, she retained an old-world charm that men admired and respected. Yet one of her friends also added, "Men took orders from her—even Liberian men—when they wouldn't take that from any other woman."

The party now moving slowly up hill and down, through swamps and across rivers, had grown to about 50 people. Gus had approached his friends, the De La Haye's at Radio ELWA, to come along on this missionary journey. Besides the SIM missionaries and their friends, there was Gus and his wife and four children (the youngest, Sophie, just a babe in arms) and Mother Eliza, who had returned for another visit earlier in the year.

When the Gbaizon church learned that the team was on its way, they sent a delegation of 40 people to meet them at the end of the road to help carry their supplies and accompany them back on the three-day walk into the interior.

To Mother this was an almost-unbelievable miracle, though she had depended on miracles all her life. During these 54 years in Africa, her heart's desire had been to go further into the interior to preach to lost souls who had never heard the gospel.

That's why she had moved Kelton farther away from Lexington than the townspeople wanted her to; that's why she wouldn't move the mission to Monrovia, as the Baptists had wanted her to; that's why she kept sending her children out as missionaries at great personal sacrifice (and some said to the detriment of her own work at the mission). She had never lost her vision for the natives, who had so long been excluded from the good things of earth and heaven.

And so she drank in the joyful, rhythmic singing of the porters, and the cheers and ululations as they entered a village. To sleep again in the chief's hut as a privileged and honored guest in the village brought back memories of her first treks, when she and Susie had worked together at BIA.

Wherever they stopped in the evenings the villagers gathered in their simple church "shelters," decorated with palm fronds and wild flowers. Though the people all sat on logs or bamboo poles, the honored guests were given chairs or benches at the front of the church, and then out of their simple fare they brought gifts of love—chickens, fruit, rice, and even a billy goat.

There were many speeches, but the people listened most attentively when the "God-woman" whom they had heard so much about would get up to speak.

"Children, Jesus bore the cross for you. I've seen missionaries following Jesus bearing His cross. Every one of them could have been comfortable at home.

"Africa gave birth to black people . . . I'm not ashamed of being black. My mother said to me, 'Liza, if I was a black man, I would go back to Africa.' When I was in my mother's womb, she said she had a longing to come to Africa . . . it came out in me. I love Africa . . . if I had a thousand lives, I'd give them all to God for Africa.

"Pray for our people in America. They are . . . busy accumulating things, which are just for time and not for eternity."

When Eliza challenged her listeners to pray, it was not an idle cliche. She believed in two basic solutions to all her problems and had followed this simple plan all her life: every situation and every need was immediately taken to her heavenly Father in prayer. While other people slept, Eliza prayed; when crises called for fast decisions, Eliza prayed; and when things got tougher than usual, she fasted. Her children recall that at one very difficult period at the mission Mother fasted for 11 days, then got up from her bed and walked to Greenville for supplies.

Eliza loved the jungle, and she never feared its treachery. Even on this trip into Gbaizon she was undaunted by the heat and obstacles. The porters carried her though 26 swamps and 18 streams on the three-day journey. But she would just as happily have gotten down from her hammock and forded them by "ankle express" if they would have allowed it. At one point she did have to make her way across a wide river where a big tree had been felled to span the distance. The porters could not balance the hammock across the log, so Mother sat astride the "bridge" and worked her way across herself.

Eliza was to visit Africa one more time in 1972, when Dr. William Tolbert, by then President of Liberia, would personally decorate her "for distinguished and sacrificial services . . . for more than 50 long years as a missionary, teacher, mother, and friend . . . who struggled for the redemption of man's sick soul at countless cost . . . a faithful servant in the Master's vineyard."

But nothing would give her greater joy than his journey into Gbaizon, to know that the gospel had spread to the very heart of Liberia, and to see her spiritual son leading the way.

There were difficult times in the later years as Gus and Mother struggled over the direction of the work. It is never easy to turn your life's work over to someone younger, even if it is your own son, and to allow him to bring changes that seem unwise or revolutionary. But in her heart Mother knew that Gus was God's man for ENI.

At sundown on the third day the procession arrived at its final destination, and Sophie De La Haye, the SIM missionary who traveled with the party, vividly described what transpired:

"With hundreds arriving from all the surrounding villages, the town was literally turned upside down. The church was packed to overflowing, not only with the 600 women who had invited us women to come, but also with their husbands and children, who came along too.

"No one present will ever forget the service on the second evening. We visitors, seated on the platform along with Gus, Mother Eliza, Otheliah, and several of the leaders, sensed an undercurrent of excitement.

"At a certain point in the meeting Gus turned to Mother Eliza, seated beside him, and said, 'Mother, my people are in darkness. Can you give me light to share with them?'

"Then we saw that they had arranged this between them.

"Mother Eliza took a candle out of her pocket, lit it, and then lit the candle Gus was holding in his hand.

"Turning to the pastor beside him, Philip Pajebo, he lit his.

"Then we noticed that everyone had candles. The light quickly spread from one to another—to the choir, then down the rows of men, women, and children seated on mud benches and in the aisles. A little girl sitting on one of the open windows held her lit candle high . . . hundreds of candles burning brightly revealed smiling, joyful faces. What a sight—I'll never forget it!"

Tears were streaming down Mother Eliza's cheeks as she realized what her little light had done, just like the chorus she had so often taught her children—"This Little Light of Mine."

Philip turned to Mother to say, "We're thankful to you tonight that you didn't hide your light under a bed."

Then Mother turned to the crowd and began speaking. "Many times I've been lost in the night in the jungle, when only one little candle could have shown me the way . . . . It's wonderful to think that one little candle I've lit—Gus—has already lit so many others. How I praise the Lord for these lights! I'll go back home to the States talking about them."

Turning to Gus, she said, "Son, I'm so glad that when we sent you away to study, you did not lose your vision for your own people. Praise God that you have returned to help your people in Liberia."

Smiling into his eyes, Mother took his hand and pressed it warmly as their love for each other and for their Lord bound them in an even-deeper understanding of what God had done for them. There would still be struggles in the years ahead, but at this solemn moment Mother knew that she had turned the torch over to him once and for all, and that he would carry it bravely into the darkness.

chapter thirty

Year 100

Mother Eliza returned to Texas to continue her deputation schedule. At one of her last meetings, in Dallas, at 99 years of age, she spoke to a banquet of young blacks, challenging them to mission work. In her own dramatic way she threw her cane down on the platform and strutted across the stage unaided as if to say, "See, if I can still do it, you can."

Several months later she broke her lip. Her adopted daughter, Cecelia, moved her and Jenny Belle to a nursing home in Austin so the two old ladies could be closer to her. Cecelia visited Mother and Aunt Jenny every day, frequently bringing a bag of candy, which Mother loved so much. Mother was alert and loved by everyone in the home.

On January 20, 1979, Mother celebrated her hundredth birthday. She was able to leave the nursing home and attend a gala festivity at the local Baptist church, where she even gave a speech.

But 12,000 miles away, in Greenville, Liberia, a far greater celebration was taking place. Hundreds of Mother's children gathered for a great centennial celebration. A colorful parade wound through the city streets, led by a band and people carrying banners.

> ONCE YOU KNOW HER, YOU'LL NEVER FORGET HER—
> MOTHER ELIZA GEORGE, THE GREAT MISSIONARY OF THIS CENTURY

Another read:

> GREAT DAUGHTER OF AMERICA
> GREAT DESCENDANT OF AFRICA
> GREAT SAINT AND MISSIONARY MOTHER

And a third:

> HER LIFE WAS THE BEST COMMENTARY OF THE BIBLE WE HAVE EVER READ
> THE LIFE OF ELIZA DAVIS-GEORGE

Speech after speech followed as those whose lives she had touched shared in the celebration: Newspaper George, former commissioner of Tarjuoville; Philip Pajibo, head of the Gbaizon church; Moses Pajebo, principal of Sinoe high school; Gus Marwieh, director of ENI; Benjamin Jlay, private secretary to the President of Liberia; Daniel Saywiah, magistrate of Juarzon; Jacob Slah, principal of CNEC high school; Edward Kofi, commissioner of Sanquin Municipality; Tom Bestman, teacher; and many others.

The Gbaizon choir was there too, all the way from the interior to add their voices to the celebration.

A message was read from Dr. William Tolbert, and a third decoration was conferred upon Mother Eliza George:

> In consideration of sacrificial and selfless services rendered which are deserving of honor, merit, and distinction, I do hereby confer upon
>
> Eliza Davis-George
>
> the grade of *Dame Grand Commander* in the most venerable order of Knighthood of the pioneers of the Republic of Liberia.

But of all the speeches and honors, Mother would probably have been most delighted to hear of the development of the work she had begun.

> Baptist Industrial Academy—now a Liberian Baptist boarding school
>
> National Baptist Mission (the new Kelton)—ten churches (association with National Baptist Mission Board, U.S.A.)
>
> Liberian Baptists in Sinoe—Eliza Davis George Pastor's Training School—50 churches (with Southern Baptist help)
>
> ENI mission—five primary schools, one high school, one technical school (under Gus Marwieh's leadership and CNEC assistance)
>
> Independent Churches of Africa—100 churches (under Gus's leadership and CNEC assistance)

No doubt Mother now knows of these honors and growth of her work, but she did not learn of it while in Texas. A few days after her hundredth birthday she was rushed to the hospital with pneumonia.

Cecelia stayed at her side, but she realized that Mother had decided that "100 is long enough."

On March 8, 1979, Mother Eliza Davis-George went home to the heaven she had told so many people about during her long life.